STUDIES IN ECONOMIC AND SOCIAL HISTORY

This series, specially commissioned by the Economic History Society, provides a guide to the current interpretations of the key themes of economic and social history in which advances have recently been made or in which there has been significant debate.

Originally entitled 'Studies in Economic History', in 1974 the series had its scope extended to include topics in social history, and the new series title, 'Studies in Economic and Social History', signalises this development.

The series gives readers access to the best work done, helps them to draw their own conclusions in major fields of study, and by means of the critical bibliography in each book guides them in the selection of further reading. The aim is to provide a springboard to further work rather than a set of pre-packaged conclusions or short-cuts.

ECONOMIC HISTORY SOCIETY

The Economic History Society, which numbers over 3000 members, publishes the *Economic History Review* four times a year (free to members) and holds an annual conference. Enquiries about membership should be addressed to the Assistant Secretary, Economic History Society, Peterhouse, Cambridge. Full-time students may join at special rates.

STUDIES IN ECONOMIC AND SOCIAL HISTORY

Edited for the Economic History Society by L. A. Clarkson

PUBLISHED

W. I. Albert Latin America and the World Economy from Independence to 1930
B. W. E. Alford Depression and Recovery? British Economic Growth, 1918–1939
Michael Anderson Approaches to the History of the Western Family, 1500–1914
P. J. Cain Economic Foundations of British Overseas Expansion, 1815–1914
S. D. Chapman The Cotton Industry in the Industrial Revolution
Neil Charlesworth British Rule and the Indian Economy, 1800–1914
J. A. Chartres Internal Trade in England, 1500–1700
R. A. Church The Great Victorian Boom, 1850–1873
L. A. Clarkson Proto-Industrialization: The First Phase of Industrialization?
D. C. Coleman Industry in Tudor and Stuart England
P. L. Cottrell British Overseas Investment in the Nineteenth Century
Ralph Davis English Overseas Trade, 1500–1700
Ian M. Drummond The Gold Standard and the International Monetary System
M. E. Falkus The Industrialisation of Russia, 1700–1914
Peter Fearon The Origins and Nature of the Great Slump, 1929–1932
T. R. Gourvish Railways and the British Economy, 1830–1914
Robert Gray The Aristocracy of Labour in Nineteenth-century Britain, c 1850–1900
John Hatcher Plague, Population and the English Economy, 1348–1530
J. R. Hay The Origins of the Liberal Welfare Reforms, 1906–1914
R. H. Hilton The Decline of Serfdom in Medieval England
E. L. Jones The Development of English Agriculture, 1815–1973
John Lovell British Trade Unions, 1875–1933
W. J. Macpherson The Economic Development of Japan, c 1868–1941
Donald N. McCloskey Econometric History
Hugh McLeod Religion and the Working Class in Nineteenth-Century Britain
J. D. Marshall The Old Poor Law, 1795–1834
Alan S. Milward The Economic Effects of the Two World Wars on Britain
G. E. Mingay Enclosure and the Small Farmer in the Age of the Industrial Revolution
Rosalind Mitchison British Population Change Since 1860
R. J. Morris Class and Class Consciousness in the Industrial Revolution, 1780–1850
J. Forbes Munro Britain in Tropical Africa, 1870–1960
A. E. Musson British Trade Unions, 1800–1875
R. B. Outhwaite Inflation in Tudor and Early Stuart England
R. J. Overy The Nazi Economic Recovery, 1932–1938
P. L. Payne British Entrepreneurship in the Nineteenth Century
Roy Porter Disease, Medicine and Society in England, 1550–1860
G. D. Ramsay The English Woollen Industry, 1500–1750
Michael E. Rose The Relief of Poverty, 1834–1914
Michael Sanderson Education, Economic Change and Society in England, 1780–1870
S. B. Saul The Myth of the Great Depression, 1873–1896
Arthur J. Taylor Laissez-faire and State Intervention in Nineteenth-century Britain
Peter Temin Causal Factors in American Economic Growth in the Nineteenth Century
Joan Thirsk England's Agricultural Regions and Agrarian History, 1500–1750
Michael Turner Enclosures in Britain, 1750–1830
Margaret Walsh The American Frontier Revisited
J. R. Ward Poverty and Progress in the Caribbean 1800–1960

OTHER TITLES ARE IN PREPARATION

Keynes, The Treasury and British Economic Policy

Prepared for
The Economic History Society by

G. C. Peden
Reader in Economic and Social History
University of Bristol

MACMILLAN
EDUCATION

First published 1988

Published by
MACMILLAN EDUCATION LTD
Houndmills, Basingstoke, Hampshire RG21 2XS
and London
Companies and representatives
throughout the world

Printed in Hong Kong

British Library Cataloguing in Publication Data
Peden, G. C.
Keynes, the Treasury and British economic
policy.——(Studies in economic and
social history).
1. Keynes, John Maynard 2. Great Britain
——Economic policy—1918–1945
I.   Title II. Economic History Society
III.   Series
330.941'083   HB99.7
ISBN   0–333–36272–1

Series Standing Order

If you would like to receive future titles in this series as they are
published, you can make use of our standing order facility. To place a
standing order please contact your bookseller or, in case of difficulty,
write to us at the address below with your name and address and the
name of the series. Please state with which title you wish to begin your
standing order. (If you live outside the United Kingdom we may not
have the rights for your area, in which case we will forward your order
to the publisher concerned.)

Customer Services Department, Macmillan Distribution Ltd
Houndmills, Basingstoke, Hampshire, RG21 2XS, England.

Contents

Acknowledgements

I am grateful to Susan Howson, Neil Rollings and Robert Skidelsky, and an unknown reader, for constructive criticism; to Sir Alec Cairncross and Neil Rollings for the opportunity to read forthcoming works; and to Rosemary Graham, Anne Griffiths and Anita Hathway for their skill in producing the typescript.

Note on References

References in the text within square brackets relate to the numbered items in the Bibliography, followed, where necessary, by the page numbers in italics, for example (1: *7–9*).

Editor's Preface

WHEN this series was established in 1968 the first editor, the late Professor M. W. Flinn, laid down three guiding principles. The books should be concerned with important fields of economic history; they should be surveys of the current state of scholarship rather than a vehicle for the specialist views of the authors, and above all, they were to be introductions to their subject and not 'a set of pre-packaged conclusions'. These aims were admirably fulfilled by Professor Flinn and by his successor, Professor T. C. Smout, who took over the series in 1977. As it passes to its third editor and approaches its third decade, the principles remain the same.

Nevertheless, times change, even though principles do not. The series was launched when the study of economic history was burgeoning and new findings and fresh interpretations were threatening to overwhelm students – and sometimes their teachers. The series has expanded its scope, particularly in the area of social history – although the distinction between 'economic' and 'social' is sometimes hard to recognize and even more diffficult to sustain. It has also extended geographically; its roots remain firmly British, but an increasing number of titles is concerned with the economic and social history of the wider world. However, some of the early titles can no longer claim to be introductions to the current state of scholarship; and the discipline as a whole lacks the heady growth of the 1960s and early 1970s. To overcome the first problem a number of new editions, or entirely new works, have been commissioned – some have already appeared. To deal with the second, the aim remains to publish up-to-date introductions to important areas of debate. If the series can demonstrate to students and their teachers the importance of the discipline of economic and social history and excite its further study, it will continue the task so ably begun by its first two editors.

The Queen's University of Belfast L. A. CLARKSON
General Editor

1 Introduction

JOHN Maynard Keynes was the most influential British economist of the twentieth century. He produced a new analytical framework through which economists and policy–makers could view the problems of unemployment and inflation. Although the Keynesian consensus which emerged in the economics profession in the 1940s has been challenged since the late 1960s by monetarist theories, the writer of this pamphlet is not alone in believing that Keynes was the best source of economic advice available during the interwar years and down to his death in 1946. Indeed, until recently most economic accounts of that period have been written from a more-or-less Keynesian point of view. However, this should not be taken to imply that there were no practical impediments to government acceptance of Keynes's advice. This pamphlet seeks to contrast Keynes's ideas with the alternative wisdom emanating from the Treasury, the department responsible for drawing up the budget, for controlling central-government expenditure and, in conjunction with the Bank of England, for managing the National Debt. There has been an extended debate in recent years about Keynes's influence on the Treasury. This debate has at least had the merit of bringing out more clearly than before the arguments deployed by Treasury officials against Keynes and others who advocated expansionary economic policies. These arguments help to place Keynes in historical perspective. They also make a contribution to our understanding of the problem of unemployment in the interwar period, and also to our understanding of the nature of the 'Keynesian revolution' which, according to standard texts, took place in economic policy during or shortly after the Second World War [31: *58, 178–87*; 92: *159–72*; 137: *185–8*].

There were in fact two distinct 'Keynesian revolutions', one in economic theory and the other in economic policy. Although our chief concern will be with the latter, it has to be seen on the context of the former. Keynes wrote two major works on economic theory: *A Treatise on Money* (1930) and *The General Theory of Employment,*

Interest and Money (1936). In the *Treatise* Keynes tried to show that not all savings found their way into capital outlay (as orthodox economics then taught). He was, however, disappointed by the response of the economics profession to the *Treatise* and he set out in the *General Theory* to convert his fellow professionals to his views. By the 1940s he had succeeded, so far as the younger generation of economists was concerned. As we shall see, however, this did not imply a ready conversion of Treasury officials.

The nature and significance of Keynes's contribution to economic theory has spawned an immense literature, [1] to which it is impossible to do justice in a short pamphlet on economic policy. Keynes himself stressed the novelty of his ideas by contrasting his *General Theory* with an over-simplified summary of what other economists had taught. According to Keynes, classical or pre-Keynesian economics had been founded on the notion, known as Say's Law, that supply creates its own demand: that is, the income from making all the goods and services in an economy creates the effective demand for an equal value of goods and services [78: *18–21*]. There could, in this view, be unemployment in particular industries, owing to changes in taste or technology, but there could be no general deficiency of demand and, assuming flexible prices and wages, the adjustments necessary to restore full employment could be left to market forces. However, within the classical economic literature there was a host of amendments to the basic model, and by the end of the 1920s the vast majority of British economists was in favour of the temporary adoption of expansionist policies as remedies' for unemployment in times of exceptional depressions [27; 65: *121–99*]. What Keynes could with some justice claim to have done in the *General Theory* was to have replaced the tattered classical version of an economy which was stable in the long run, with a vision of an economy prone to overproduction and secular stagnation, with full employment being a special case rather than the rule. Classical economics had implied that governments could, and indeed except in exceptional circumstances should, remain neutral influences on the economy, matching expenditure with revenue. Keynesian economics implied that governments must accept permanent responsibility for aggregate demand in the economy, to ensure that it was sufficient to secure full employment without, however, producing a vicious spiral of rising prices and wages. Aggregate demand could be managed in various ways, but Keynes stressed that governments should be willing to borrow to finance their expenditure when the economy was at less than full employment.

The Keynesian revolution in economic theory was a long-drawn-out process. Keynes spent over six years writing the *Treatise*, and drafts show that his ideas were continually changing over that period. The *General Theory* took almost four years to write, beginning in 1932, and its composition was described by Keynes as a long struggle of escape ... from habitual modes of thought' [78: *xxiii*]. The *Treatise* itself did not show by how much output and employment would change when there were changes in aggregate demand. It was left to Kahn, with his concept of the multiplier (see Chapter 3 below) to develop from ideas in the *Treatise* the concept of the supply curve of total output. This supply curve was designed to show the extent to which changes in demand would lead to price changes on the one hand, and changes in output and employment on the other. Using the concept of the multiplier, Keynes showed how a flow of government expenditure could raise national income, and therefore create the savings from which government loans could be subscribed, as well as raising tax revenue (98). If the multiplier were large enough, there might be no net cost to the government (this point is taken up in Chapter 3).

As Skidelsky [134] has pointed out, the 'Keynesian revolution' in policy involved more than changes in economic theory: new attitudes were also required to Britain's role in the international economy and the state's role in the national economy. The British economy had become so enmeshed in the international economy during the nineteenth century that after the First World War British policy-makers were inclined to believe that measures to improve international finance and trade must benefit Britain, even if the cost were to be large price and wage adjustments within Britain. Keynes was no opponent of international co-operation, but he was to argue that, as in the case of the return to the gold standard in 1925, the cost could be too high (see Chapter 2). Even more fundamental was his battle with the so-called 'Treasury view', which defended a minimalist role for the state with the argument that government expenditure was unproductive, serving only to deplete the stock of capital available for investment. This issue did turn in part on the theoretical points raised in the *Treatise* and the *General Theory*, but it also involved administrative and political questions, which may have been of decisive importance to the Treasury (see

Chapter 3). Keynes was inclined to assume that economic policy could be directed by non-political experts, using powers of persuasion [48: *192–3*]. The Treasury, on the other hand, was inclined to stress the practical problems of regulating public expenditure and also, anticipating modern critics of Keynes such as Buchanan, Burton and Wagner [17], to believe that politicians, if released from the discipline of the balanced budget, would be more interested in competing for electoral favour by spending money than in following the advice of economic experts.

The contrasts in personalities and roles between Keynes and Treasury officials are worth some attention. Keynes's character was by no means fully revealed by his first biographer, Harrod [136: *xv–xxiii*]. At the time of writing, two new biographies are being prepared by Moggridge and Skidelsky, but meanwhile the best short assessment is probably that by Elizabeth Johnson [67]. Keynes was not only a serious social scientist but also a vigorous pamphleteer who believed that 'words ought to be a little wild, for they are the assault of thoughts upon the unthinking' [84: *244*]. Wild words could, however, provoke resentment among those at whom they were directed, and even Sir Frederick Phillips, a Treasury official who was sympathetic to Keynes's arguments, could complain of 'Keynes's customary optimism, over-emphasis and neglect of ulterior consequences' [104: *181*]. Treasury officials were too sceptical by nature and training to be easily swayed by Keynes's optimism concerning new economic remedies. There is, no doubt, a tendency for all civil servants to use accumulated departmental wisdom and practical philosophy to temper ministerial enthusiasm for new ideas [14]. In the Treasury's case, this tendency was reinforced by the department's responsibility for controlling central-government expenditure, from the point of view of value for money as well as broad aggregates [15; 16; 117; 128]. This responsibility had been underlined in 1919 by the decision of the government to make the Permanent Secretary (official head) of the Treasury, Sir Warren Fisher, also the official head of the Civil Service – a step designed to give the Treasury the means by which it could control other departments [18: *98–9*]. The Treasury's power over the purse strings lapsed during the Second World War, when the physical allocation of productive resources, including manpower, determined what finance had to be provided. The Treasury's eventual acceptance of Keynesian demand management – in so far as this was

accepted – was probably not unconnected with the fact that acceptance would restore the centrality of finance, and therefore of the
Treasury, in the conduct of economic policy (see Chapter 7).

Keynes recognised that the Treasury was the central department
of government in the interwar period, and he made it the focus of
his attempts to influence opinion in Whitehall. He was, of course,
also very much interested in influencing the Bank of England,
especially in the period 1921–31 when it was given a free hand, at
least in principle, to operate bank rate without political interference
[58; 91: 95–6; 132]. Nevertheless, it was with the Treasury that
Keynes had his strongest links. He had served in the Treasury as
a civil servant from 1915 to 1919, and he was consulted by chancellors from time to time thereafter, before returning to the Treasury
as an adviser between 1940 and his death in 1946. Keynes believed
that practical men were 'usually the slaves of some defunct economist' [78: 383] and tried to educate leading Treasury officials in
various ways, for example through the Tuesday Club, an informal
gathering of economists, City men and civil servants. How far
Treasury officials were slaves of any economist remains uncertain,
however. The Treasury avoided putting its views in the form of
theoretical doctrine [83: 172], and in any case Treasury views varied
both as between officials and over time. Only one Treasury official
in the interwar period, Ralph Hawtrey, had the reputation of being
an economist. Hawtrey saw the trade cycle as largely a monetary
phenomenon, which led him to advocate a 'cheap money' policy of
low interest rates from 1921, but his theory also led him to regard
Keynes's favourite remedy for unemployment, public works, as
unnecessary. Hawtrey believed that, except in exceptional circumstances, the Bank of England could achieve the same effect as public
works on employment by stimulating private investment through
credit expansion [52]. Hawtrey published his ideas extensively at
the time, but it has only been through painstaking research into
the Treasury's own records that Howson has been able to show
when leading officials agreed with Hawtrey and when they did not.
Hawtrey's ideas were used in support of Treasury arguments against
public works in the 1920s, but his influence waned in the 1930s
[58; 59; 62; 63].

Much else has been learned about the Treasury's ideas about
policy from study of the department's own records, which have
been released under the 30 Year Rule, Moggridge [105] being the

first to use this source in 1969. Previously the Treasury's ideas had to be deduced from sparse official statements on particular issues, for Treasury officials from the period who had published memoirs [45; 91] had not cast much light on official thought. The comparative richness of the Treasury and Cabinet Office source material available since the late 1960s has encouraged a re-interpretation of the 1920s, 30s and 40s. Whereas previously economic historians had tended to be strongly influenced by Keynes's published works, sometimes taking the 'wild words' of his polemical writings too literally, it was now possible to follow the debate in Whitehall. In the works of Howson [58] or Middleton [104], for example, in contrast to some older Keynesian accounts (e.g. Winch [150] in 1969) the Treasury is portrayed as neither monolithic nor obscurantist. Likewise, the appearance of hitherto unpublished material in the Royal Economic Society's edition of *The Collected Writings of John Maynard Keynes* has also had the effect of softening earlier judgements, since in private Keynes's words were often less 'wild' than when he was trying to influence public opinion

It is also likely that some economic historians have been influenced by events since the 1970s. The experience on stagflation has cast a shadow over the prestige of Keynesian economics, and consequently the earlier assumption that Keynes had the answer to unemployment [137: *13*] no longer readily finds acceptance. Increasing attention is now paid to structural aspects of unemployment, and this too has tended to dispel a belief in easy Keynesian answers [11; 41].

Ideally debate on the 'Keynesian revolution' in economic policy would be centred on a single model of what such a revolution would imply. However, given that Keynes's ideas were evolving through the 1920s, 30s and 40s this is not possible. Instead it seems best to suggest five areas in which a 'Keynesian revolution' could have taken place at various times. These are, firstly, international monetary policy; secondly, domestic monetary policy; thirdly, the use of public investment as a means of creating employment; fourthly, the use of Keynes's macroeconomic concepts; fifthly, fiscal policy.

Keynes first made his mark as an advocate of a managed currency in the 1920s. This was in contrast to the monetary authorities (the Treasury and the Bank of England) who wished to restore the supposedly automatic gold standard, whereby domestic interest rates, and, in theory, investment levels, prices and wages, were determined by the need to maintain a fixed exchange rate. Keynes believed in price stability, and he appreciated that stable exchange rates benefited international finance and trade, but he believed that domestic price stability must have priority, and that therefore the exchange rate must be flexible [76]. The more Keynes became concerned with unemployment, the stronger grew his belief that maintenance of the exchange rate should not inhibit investment. However, after Britain had returned to the gold standard in 1925, he was careful not to advocate a deliberate act of devaluation, as such an act would be a shock to international finance [95: 110–11]. Once Britain had been forced off the gold standard in 1931, he argued that the exchange rate should be chosen to enable a domestic monetary policy of low, stable interest rates to be carried out. International co-operation was desirable, however, and Keynes sought to reconcile his domestic and international monetary objectives through the Bretton Woods system of stable, but adjustable, exchange rates.

Change and consistency are also to be found in Keynes's ideas on domestic monetary policy [109]. In 1920, during the postwar inflationary boom, and in the absence of other controls, Keynes was an advocate of a very high bank rate, to moderate businessmen's expectations about profits [56]. In the *Treatise*, however, he emphasised the importance of the long-term rate of interest rather than bank rate as the focus of policy. In contrast to Hawtrey, who continued to believe in the immediate efficacy of bank rate [53], Keynes had come to believe that the volume of investment in working capital was relatively inelastic to changes in the short-term rate of interest (although a rise in the latter would, of course, raise the long-term rate). In the post-1929 slump Keynes argued that monetary policy alone could not bring about recovery, because businessmen were so pessimistic that they would respond to low interest rates only after the state had increased economic activity through public investment. Subsequently, as private investment recovered down to 1937, he stressed the need to find means other than raising bank rate to prevent a boom getting out of hand, on the grounds that, once the monetary authorities made money dearer, they would find it hard to reverse the trend.

Keynes's emphasis on public investment as an employment policy was originally focused in the 1920s on 'public works', such as roads and electrical transmission lines, financed by loans outside the chancellor's budget. However, public works were seen as short–term stimuli to private investment, rather than as a programme of long-term public investment designed permanently to raise the level of economic activity. In the *General Theory*, in the context of a long–term prospect of inadequate private investment, Keynes wrote of the need for 'comprehensive socialisation' of investment, but this apparently meant no more than management by the state of the aggregate level of investment, and did not imply nationalisation [78: *378*]. Keynes believed that the state would know what total investment should be, if it used a national income accounting framework. National income accounting was already being developed by economists before the 'Keynesian revolution' as represented by the *General Theory* [111; 142: *129–30*]. However, apart from an unpublished exercise by the Inland Revenue in 1929 [138], no official national income statistics were compiled in Britain before 1940/41, and willingness to employ the macroeconomic concepts of the *General Theory* is an important litmus test of official adoption of Keynes's ideas.

Fiscal policy, which might seem to be the essence of the post-war 'Keynesian revolution', was barely mentioned in the *General Theory*. Earlier loan-financed public works schemes had implied temporary budget deficits, but most of the expenditure would have been by local authorities or public corporations outside the chancellor's budget, as then conventionally defined. It was in his *How to Pay for the War* (1940) that Keynes decisively shifted his emphasis to fiscal policy, with a view to preventing inflation. Keynes did carry the Treasury with him in this context in the 1941 budget but it can be argued that an important test of a 'Keynesian revolution' in economic policy relates to a willingness to use fiscal policy to tackle unemployment. Certainly it is on this test that some of the most recent debate over Keynes and the Treasury has been focused.

2 International Monetary Policy

OF the five areas in which one may test whether and when a 'Keynesian revolution' took place – international monetary policy, domestic monetary policy, public investment as an employment policy, macroeconomic concepts and fiscal policy – it is convenient to consider the first on its own before looking at the others. It was over the return to the gold standard in 1925 that Keynes had one of his most celebrated disagreements with the Treasury, but there was a considerable convergence of views after Britain left the gold standard in 1931. During the Second World War Keynes was the Treasury's principal negotiator in the talks leading to the Bretton Woods agreements, which laid the basis of the post-war international monetary system. It is the broad measure of agreement between Keynes and the Treasury on international monetary policy after 1931 which makes continued differences over domestic economic policy all the more striking.

The nature of the international gold standard, and its disruption during and after the First World War, are the subject of another pamphlet in this series [33]. Britain officially left the gold standard, which had virtually been in suspense since 1914, in March 1919. It was not until December of that year that the chancellor of the exchequer, Austen Chamberlain, announced that the government had accepted the recommendations of the Cunliffe Committee [28]. These were a cessation of government borrowing, the exercise of economy in public expenditure and a limit to the issue of currency notes – all measures designed to lead to a return to the pre-1914 gold standard [57].

There is widespread agreement among economic historians that Britain's return to the gold standard in 1925, at the 1914 price of gold, was an error. Even Winston Churchill, the chancellor who took the final decision on the advice of Treasury officials and the Bank of England, subsequently became convinced of this. Restoring the gold value of sterling fixed the exchange rate in relation to all other currencies based on gold, and Keynes warned in 1925 that

17

the chosen rate was too high to be sustained without deflation. In his view this meant deliberate intensification of unemployment until wages and prices adjusted [79: *207–30*]. Keynes also warned that while a general return to the international gold standard would stabilise exchange rates, it would not guarantee stability of prices, since world prices had been far from stable, even in the United States, which had remained on the gold standard. Keynes therefore advocated a managed currency, with an exchange rate which would be adjustable in the interests of internal price stability [76]. The issues to be discussed here with reference to the gold standard are: (a) was Keynes right in his estimate of the extent of sterling's overvaluation and its effects? and (b) how viable was his alternative of a managed currency?

The broad lines of domestic monetary policy in the period are well covered in the works of Howson [58] and Morgan [110]. The banking system emerged from the war flush with cash and liquid assets, and there was an inflationary boom in 1919–20, following the relaxation of wartime controls on investment. Keynes at this time fully supported those in the Treasury who called for higher interest rates and monetary restriction to break inflation, and indeed he said in 1942 that, in the absence of physical controls over investment, he would give the same advice again [56]. Restrictive monetary measures came at a time when business optimism was giving way to doubt, and a deep slump followed. Meanwhile the exchange rate, which had stood at $4.86 before the war, and at about $4.76 during the war, fell sharply during the post-war inflation, to a low of $3.40 in February 1920, and then recovered in the slump, reaching $4.63 late in 1922. Keynes thought that the Treasury's policy of returning to the pre-1914 par was a mistake, but he urged that if that was to be our policy then the return should be swift, to avoid a long-drawn-out deflation [82: *61*]. The Treasury, however, preferred to wait in the vain hope that a rise in American prices would bring the exchange to par, and a long-drawn-out deflation resulted.

The story of the final decision to return has been carefully documented by Moggridge [105: *25–68*; 106: *37–97*] on the basis of the Treasury's records, and his account has been confirmed independently by Sayers [132: vol. 1, *134*], who had full access to the records of the Bank of England. Keynes was called as a witness before the Treasury's Committee on the Currency and Bank of

England Note Issues (the Chamberlain–Bradbury Committee) in 1924, and he was consulted informally by Churchill early in 1925. The latter was sufficiently impressed by Keynes's arguments as to require full statements for the case for gold from Sir Otto Niemeyer, his leading Treasury adviser, Hawtrey and Montagu Norman, the governor of the Bank of England. Niemeyer's reply is interesting for its claim that unemployment could only be dealt with by measures to improve trade (rather than by public works) and that the gold standard would improve international trade, by stabilising exchange rates. At this date Niemeyer thought that the difference between British and American prices was only 4 per cent and that 'no very heroic steps' would be needed to maintain gold parity with the dollar [106: 262–9].

Subsequent discussion of the effects of the return to gold has been dominated by Keynes's polemical pamphlet, *The Economic Consequences of Mr. Churchill* [79: 207–30], which was published only three months after the event. Although Ashworth [6: 387] has remarked that most price figures indicate that Keynes was exaggerating when estimating the extent of overvaluation at about 10 per cent, this is the figure commonly repeated by economic historians such as Constantine [26 51], Moggridge [108: 72] and Pollard [122: 137–8]. Independent work on purchasing power parities by Dimsdale [30] and Redmond [125] has tended to confirm Keynes's view that sterling was overvalued. Indeed Dimsdale estimated that taking into account changes in Gross National Product and consumers' expenditure in Britain and America since 1914, sterling's overvaluation was about 11–14 per cent, and even more if account be taken of changes in the structure of the two economies. Changes in technology, costs and consumer taste had all favoured the United States. Redmond recognises fully the difficulties in making purchasing power parity calculations, since the results will vary with the choice of price index, the choice of base year, and the allowance made for structural changes since the base year. Wholesale price indices indicate that the pound was at equilibrium in 1925; different retail price indices indicate anything from equilibrium to a 9 per cent overvaluation. It was on the basis of a comparison of changes in wholesale prices since before the war that the Treasury had calculated that sterling was overvalued by as little as $1\frac{1}{2}$ per cent in 1925, whereas Keynes's estimate was on the basis of retail prices. While Keynes himself recognised that the retail indices available were less than satisfactory [77: vol. 1, chs 4 & 5], there can be no doubt that he was right to argue against the use of wholesale price indices. Wholesale price indices included a large element of imported goods which were traded on international commodity markets and therefore had a single world price. Such indices therefore did not reflect the true internal price adjustment necessary to sustain $4.86.

Any doubts that sterling was overvalued in 1925 are removed once one considers currencies other than the dollar. The effects on British trade are best understood with reference to a 'basket' of foreign currencies, weighted according to their importance in international trade. Dimsdale [30: *317*] has produced figures showing sterling rising by 35 per cent against such a weighted basket, compared with 15 per cent against the dollar in 1921–4, and Redmond [125: *529*] has produced a variety of multilateral measures indicating a sterling overvaluation of 20–25 per cent in 1925. It is worth noting, however, that price changes and currency realignments after 1925 reduced the degree of overvaluation to 15–20 per cent by 1929.

It would seem that the British monetary authorities' failure to take into account foreign currencies other than the dollar was most culpable. Sayers [131: *321–4*] argued in mitigation that, whatever rate Britain had adopted in 1925, France and Belgium at least would each have adopted a lower one, and certainly the competitive advantage gained by sterling's depreciation after Britain left the gold standard in 1931 was quickly eroded by the depreciation or devaluation of other currencies [124]. Even so, a lower exchange rate than $4.86 in 1925 might still have helped British exports, especially of new products facing American and German competition. Germany had stabilised the mark on gold in 1924 at a lower rate than in 1914, and her subsequent re-emergence as a major trading competitor with Britain should have been foreseen. Moreover, if Commonwealth and Empire countries which pegged their currencies to sterling had kept in step with Britain, as they did when Britain left the gold standard in 1931, a significant devaluation in the 1920s should have increased the total external earnings of the sterling system [123].

It is not by any means easy to estimate what would have happened if the Treasury had accepted Keynes's contention that sterling would be overvalued at $4.86. Moggridge [105: *69–79*; 106:

245–50] attempted to do so by assuming British imports of goods to have a sterling price elasticity of demand of –0.5 (i.e. a 1 per cent fall in the sterling price of imports relative to other goods would raise the volume of imports demanded by 0.5 per cent) and British exports of goods to have a foreign currency price elasticity of demand of –1.5. On this basis, and making allowances for effects on Britain's 'invisible' account (mainly income from shipping and City of London services plus net income from international debts and investment), Moggridge reckoned that, had sterling been 10 per cent lower than $4.86 in 1928, there would have been an improvement in the current balance of payments approaching £70 million. Had this improvement reduced unemployment among insured workers from 10.8 per cent (the 1928 average) to 4.7 per cent (the pre–1914 average), 729,000 more people could have been in jobs. Assuming a marginal propensity to import of 0.3, the improved current balance of payments would have accommodated the employment of these people at wages equal to the national average net domestic income per person employed, and still have left a margin of £25 million over to finance overseas lending, increased government spending, or higher wages.

These calculations have been criticised by Alford [5: *35–6*] for using a price elasticity of demand for British exports based on experience of international trade over a long period, whereas Britain's traditional export industries – coal, cotton, iron and steel, and ship-building – all faced unusually acute difficulties of obsolescence or world overcapacity in the 1920s. The price elasticity of demand for their products was probably exceptionally low, and only a structural shift in the British economy towards new industries could have altered this. Dimsdale [30: *322*], using a low price elasticity of demand for Britsh exports of −0.5, has calculated that a 10 per cent reduction in the $4.86 exchange rate in 1928 would have raised employment by only 450,000, after four to five years, and only if wages did not rise in response to increased costs of imports. Dimsdale regards the last point as a questionable assumption, which may be so for 1928, but in fact when Britain did leave the gold standard in 1931 there was no surge of import costs or wages. This was owing to the effects of the post–1929 international depression on commodity prices, plus the fact that many of Britain's suppliers of food and raw materials linked their currencies to sterling.

The effects of the return to gold were not confined to the current account of the balance of payments. Financing the First World War had transformed Britain's short–term credit position from one of rough balance in 1914 to one where the ratio of short-term assets held by foreigners in London to short-term debts of foreigners to London was approximately 2:1. Sterling was thus vulnerable to a movement of funds from London, if interest rates were higher elsewhere, or if fund–holders felt that sterling's exchange rate would fall [110]. Achieving and maintaining a par of $4.86 thus implied a willingness to raise bank rate to a level which even Niemeyer recognised could have a detrimental effect on unemployment [58: 28]. Keynes, indeed, argued that it was by reducing credit and investment, and thereby creating unemployment, until wages and prices fell, that the gold standard mechanism worked [132: vol. 3, 179–80]. Nevertheless, Aldcroft [2: 326–34; 3], following Governor Norman, has argued that, except in 1920–1, business was not really hampered by high credit charges as a result of high bank rates. However, it is difficult not to agree with Catterall [22] that the Norman–Aldcroft view takes inadequate account of reductions in prices of capital goods, which raised real interest rates. On the other hand, it would seem that Pollard [121: 3] went too far when he suggested that the return to gold was the reason why Britain suffered from persistent mass unemployment during the 1920s while the rest of the industrial world enjoyed a boom between 1924 and 1929. Britain's structural problems were to prove too great to be readily removed by low interest rates combined with a floating exchange rate in the 1930s. Even so, the overvaluation of sterling was undoubtedly a severe blow to the export staples in the 1920s and exacerbated the depression in the regions in which these industries were concentrated [68].

Turning to Keynes's ideas on a managed currency in the early 1920s, these are set out in his *Tract on Monetary Reform* (1923) and in his evidence to the Chamberlain–Bradbury Committee in 1924 [82: 238–61]. Keynes agreed with Treasury officials, such as Hawtrey [51] that capitalist society was dependent upon contracts denominated in money. Nor was there anything in Keynes's underlying theory at this stage which would have led him to dissent from the view of Sir John Bradbury (a former joint permanent secretary of the Treasury) that monetary management which did not maintain the value of creditors' money would lead to an unwillingness to forgo consumption, and, therefore, would diminish savings, which, according to pre–Keynesian theory, would in turn diminish funds available for investment [95: 266–7]. What Keynes pointed out was that the gold standard did not guarantee stability in the value of money, except in the unlikely event of external price levels remaining stable. Moreover, the supply of new gold could only be sufficient for world monetary needs by accident. Consequently he suggested that, instead of gold, Britain's standard of value should be an official index of the composite price of commodities, weighted in accordance to their relative economic importance. One may doubt whether such an index would have been sufficiently immutable, or, if it had been, whether it would have kept touch with reality as the relative economic importance of commodities changed. However, given the degree of active monetary management required to revalue sterling from $3.40 to $4.86, one can agree with Keynes that his proposals for a managed currency were no more than an adaptation of the actual system which developed after 1919. It is not at all clear that what Keynes proposed was any more impracticable than a policy which raised British manufacturers' real wage costs at a time when money wages proved to be inflexible. Admittedly there is an element of hindsight in this judgement, since not even Keynes had anticipated in 1925 how inflexible wages would be thereafter [132: vol. 3, *179*]. Money wages had, after all, fallen by an average of 23 per cent in the deep depression of 1920–2.

The crucial difference between Keynes and Treasury officials in the 1920s over the question of a managed currency seems to have been that the latter had a less optimistic view of the ability of politicians to resist the temptation to spend once monetary discipline was relaxed. Government expenditure during the war had been financed by inflationary borrowing, and it had only been with difficulty that Lloyd George had been brought to accept restrictive monetary measures in 1919 [57]. Hyperinflation in Germany in 1922–3 strengthened the mood in favour of financial discipline. Bradbury, in a well–known phrase, described the gold standard as 'knave proof' [45: *183*]. For their part, chancellors such as Churchill and Philip Snowden defended the autonomy of the Bank of England under the gold standard, as this removed from the government responsibility for movements in interest rates [142: *98, 150*; 148: *105–6, 110*]. In the 1930s, however, Neville Chamberlain, as chancellor, was to show that fiscal orthodoxy could survive a regimen

23

of floating exchange rates, while both government and business benefited from the cheap money which such a regimen conferred (see Chapter 4).

Once Britain had been forced off the gold standard in September 1931, following a financial crisis in Europe and a political crisis at home, the Treasury had to reassess its exchange-rate policy. Keynes's advice was sought by the Treasury at the end of 1931 and his arguments were used by officials, notably Phillips, who were opposed to a return to the gold standard [58: *82–6, 173–9*]. As one might expect, Keynes was an advocate of a managed currency which would help the balance of trade and redress the fall in prices since 1929, while avoiding any vicious spiral of rising wages and prices [84: *16–29*]. These now became the Treasury's objectives. Phillips devised the Exchange Equalisation Account, which was intended to even out fluctuations in the exchange rate and, in particular, to prevent speculators forcing up sterling above the level desired by the Treasury. The Account was managed by the Bank of England on a day-to-day basis, but policy was decided in the Treasury. The Treasury hoped with the aid of its new exchange-rate policy to eliminate the deficit in the current balance of payments and to raise employment at the existing level of wages [60]. However, other countries also floated or devalued after 1931, so that British traders' competitive advantage was short-lived [124]. In particular, the US Treasury was determined to deny British exporters any competitive advantage through sterling depreciation, and made plain that it was prepared to achieve the exchange rate it desired by deliberate depreciation of the dollar, as in 1933 [32: *181–205, 214–5, 224–5, 235–51; 60; 19–23, 28, 31–2*; 118: *178*]. It would seem that the main long–term benefit from sterling's managed float was the policy of cheap money, pursued from 1932, once there was no need to raise bank rate to maintain a fixed exchange rate [20: *83–103*]. Be that as it may, the fact remains that the deficit in the current balance of payments had been eliminated by 1933, and unemployment in 1937 was half what it had been in 1932.

Keynes was well aware that competitive currency depreciations, and also exchange restrictions and tariffs, were mutually injurious if applied by all countries [79: *352*]. He was, therefore, an advocate of international co–operation. He had already in the *Treatise* sketched out ideas for an independent international central bank [77: *348–64*] and in the *Means to Prosperity* (1933) he proposed that such an international authority should issue gold notes, both to manage world prices and to provide the liquidity for increased loan–financed public investment throughout the world [79: *350–9*]. The Treasury did in fact adopt the idea of raising world prices through an international note issue, but it was opposed to participation in an international programme of public works. In any event, neither proposal won acceptance at the World Economic Conference in 1933 [63: *116–21*].

The experience of beggar-my-neighbour policies in the 1930s gave a strong impetus during the Second World War for Anglo–American discussions on international measures to provide protection against wild fluctuations in prices, exchange rates, trade and employment. Keynes was one of the principal authors of the Bretton Woods agreements of 1944, which led to the establishment of the International Monetary Fund (IMF). However, in the 1940s Keynes was no longer simply offering advice: he was actively engaged in negotiations with the Americans as the British Treasury's representative. It is well known that in almost every case where Keynes's views were different from those of the Americans, the American view prevailed, and that in consequence there was a much less expansionary bias to the post–war international monetary system than Keynes had hoped for. In particular, the IMF provided only a fraction of the international reserves that Keynes had proposed, and Keynes had to fight hard for Britain to retain the right to propose devaluation – and even then only to correct a 'fundamental disequilibrium' [146; 147]. Indeed so much did the Americans get their way that in 1946 Keynes doubted the wisdom of recommending the British government to ratify the Bretton Woods agreements [71].

This raises the question of why he nevertheless did so. Williamson [147] argues that there are three plausible explanations: firstly, that Keynes did not realise the extent to which his proposals had been rejected by the Americans; secondly, that he was reassured by the fact that the IMF and the World Bank were based on an intellectual consensus to which he had contributed in the 1930s; and thirdly that he was convinced that some kind of international co–operation was necessary to ensure that the United States would not withdraw into isolation once again. The last explanation would be sufficient. Britain would be dependent upon an American loan to finance essential imports in the immediate post–war period, and

25

American co–operation would be necessary to create an international environment in which British exports could expand.

In considering the debate about Keynes and the Treasury it is important to remember that assumptions about the international environment changed markedly over time. From 1925 to 1931 Keynes's proposals for domestic economic policy were calculated to make the best of a position in which Britain was committed to a fixed, overvalued exchange rate. From 1931, in the absence of a stable international monetary system, Britain's immediate best hope was a managed float which allowed expansionary domestic economic policies. During and immediately after the Second World War, however, Britain was dependent upon American aid and there was the prospect of a new international order in which Britain might prosper. Keynes and the Treasury were broadly at one regarding international monetary policy after 1931. As we shall see, however, there remained major differences over domestic economic policies.

3 Public Works as an Employment Policy

FEW economic questions have been more debated than the efficacy
or otherwise of public works as a cure for unemployment. The
contemporary arguments of the interwar years and the results of
recent historical research have been surveyed critically by Garside
[39], Middleton [104: *92–5, 144–72*] and Peden [118] and the
limited space here may therefore be devoted to two issues: (a) the
development of Keynes's ideas, and the Treasury's response; and
(b) the possible effects of implementing the policies which Keynes
advocated.

The Treasury had believed since Gladstone's time that money
was best left to 'fructify in the pockets of the people'. However, as
Skidelsky [135] pointed out, the Treasury had never had to formu-
late a theoretical defence of this view until the Gladstonian orthodoxy of minimal public expenditure was challenged during and after
the First World War. During the 1920s the Treasury developed a
doctrine that the supply of capital was limited so that when the
government borrowed in the money market it did so in competition
with industry, and thereby tended to raise interest rates and to
discourage private enterprise. Hence the famous 'Treasury view'
that 'very little additional employment and no permanent additional
employment' could be created by loan-financed public expenditure,
such as was advocated by Lloyd George in 1929.[2] (The expenditure
in question was mainly on roads, housing, telephones, electrical
transmission lines or other schemes which would produce a money
return to help pay off loans, but which would not compete with
private enterprise.)

When in 1924 Keynes first advocated public works as a cure for
unemployment, he too believed that the nation's supply of capital
was limited, and his proposals involved only a diversion of existing
funds. He suggested that the government might use revenue which
was currently being put into a Sinking Fund to repay the National
Debt, and that savings which otherwise would be invested abroad
could be borrowed [48: *345–8, 351–3*; 82; *219–23*]. By 1929 Keynes

was also taking into account the reduction in the cost of unemploy-ment relief and the increase in tax receipts from increased national income as a result of the additional work. He also hinted at the 'cumulative force of trade activity', whereby the initial state invest-ment would encourage private enterprise but, lacking a clear con-cept of the 'multiplier' he was unable to measure the effects [79: *106–7, 110–12*]. The real novelty of his position in 1929 came from his theory of the relationship between savings and investment, which he had worked out since 1924 while writing his *Treatise on Money*.

Established theory held that savings and investment were kept in equilibrium by changes in the rate of interest. However, in the *Treatise* Keynes argued that if the public increased its holdings of financial assets by more than the amount businessmen required for new capital outlay, prices would fall and businessmen would reduce output and employment. The monetary authorities should try to prevent this, by lowering the rate of interest and increasing the availability of credit. However, this might be ineffective, since the banking system had no direct control over the prices of individual commodities or over the rates of money earnings of the factors of production. Moreover there could be a conflict between external and domestic monetary policy when on the gold standard. If Britain tried to maintain a lower rate of interest than the world rate, gold would flow out of the country; but a mature economy like Britain might be unable to find profitable domestic outlets for the whole of its savings at the world rate of interest. As a solution, Keynes suggested in newspaper articles and in a pamphlet written with Hubert Henderson (*Can Lloyd George Do It?*) that the Bank of England should expand credit, and that the government should undertake loan-financed expenditure, offering a sufficient rate of interest to ensure that the new credit was invested at home and not abroad [79: *116–18*; 82: *805–12*]. Keynes believed that overseas investment did little to increase British exports of goods, whereas the Treasury was reluctant to abandon the then generally held assumption that the export of capital must ultimately be liquidated by the export of goods [100: *50–2*].

Shortly after Keynes's articles had appeared, the Conservative government published a White Paper, *Memoranda on Certain Proposals Relating to Unemployment*, in which a number of Whitehall depart-ments put forward arguments why proposals by the Liberal leader,

Lloyd George, for the expenditure of £250 million over two years on public works, were impracticable. In the Treasury's contribution the emphasis was on the administrative and other practical problems of carrying out the programme, and little space was given to the 'Treasury view' about limited capital resources. Kahn [73: *80–2*] has suggested that this switch in emphasis was a response to Keynes's articles in support of Lloyd George, in which Keynes had pointed out that if it were true that public investment could not create employment, the same must be true of private investment. Kahn offers no evidence from Treasury papers, however, and it is not clear that he or Keynes has done justice to the Treasury view. The latter seems to have depended not only upon the availability of capital but also upon an assumption that the limited range of possible forms of public investment offered relatively few profitable outlets for capital compared with private enterprise [104: *84*]. Moreover, there is now widespread agreement among economic historians that the Treasury had good reason to doubt the practicality of Lloyd George's proposals and to fear the effects of such a scheme on financial confidence [102; 103; 104: *45–56, 144–72*; 118; 142: *80–91*]. Treasury opposition to public works was not absolute – in 1928 Fisher had recommended spending £20 million over three years on roads etc. as a contribution to the solution of unemployment [3] – but officials were insistent on value for money. When the Labour government of 1929–31 embarked upon a programme of public works, the Treasury was able to limit this to schemes which would reduce costs of production and thereby make British goods more competitive on world markets [133: *180–1, 201–5*].

Keynes was able to strengthen the case for public works following Kahn's work on the multiplier in 1930 [70]. The multiplier is the ratio between the change in real income in the community and the initial change in expenditure which brought it about. For example, public expenditure on roads will lead to an increase in incomes of contractors and their suppliers and workers. The proportion of this income which is spent on British goods and services will increase the incomes of other people in the community. The multiplier effects eventually cease because savings, taxes and expenditure on imports lead to leakages from the flow of income, while rising prices reduce the real value of that income. The amount of employment created by the extra income will depend upon wage rates and the ability of the unemployed to take the jobs on offer. Keynes made use of

Colin Clark's work on national income to calculate that the multiplier was about 2 [112]. However, in his pamphlet *The Means to Prosperity* in 1933 Keynes argued that a multiplier of 1.5 would be sufficient to justify the adoption of public works which would provide a return on capital below the current rate of interest, if one also took account of reductions in unemployment relief and increases in tax receipts [79: *339–50*]. However, Treasury officials continued to be sceptical about public works and the theory of the multiplier, even although in 1935 Fisher and Sir Richard Hopkins, the two most senior Treasury officials, recommended public works of up to about £60 million to help to maintain the economic recovery then taking place [63: *130–1*; 114: *4–6*]. In 1937 an interdepartmental committee chaired by Phillips accepted Keynes's idea of varying public capital expenditure to counter a future depression. Once more, however, the figure was small in relation to Lloyd George's schemes of 1929 and 1935 for £250 million over two years: Phillips suggested a maximum difference of £50 million between a year of high expenditure and a year of low expenditure, with at least a year's delay while new projects got under way [63: *128–31*, *141–2*, *147*; 118: *176–8*]. Moreover, it seems to have been the Ministry of Labour, rather than the Treasury, which favoured the preparation of public-works programmes in readiness for a future depression, when they would be of 'real value' [93: *221–2*].

Was the Treasury justified in being so diffident towards public works once Keynes had incorporated the multiplier into his argument? Much depends upon what the multiplier effect on employment would have been, and this would have varied over time, according to shifts in the community's propensity to save or import, to changes in taxation, and to the trend of prices and wages. Some idea of the degree of variation in the multiplier effect emerges from (optimistic) estimates by Bretherton, Burchardt and Rutherford [13], with figures ranging from 1.6 in 1931 to 1.85 in 1934. Keynes himself gave different figures at different times. In the *General Theory* he estimated the multiplier to be 2.5 but a year later he thought it might be not much more than 2 at a time when, as in 1937, national income was rising and savings were probably increasing more than in proportion [78: *128*; 84: *405–6*]. Subsequent research suggests that Keynes was too optimistic. Moreover, whereas Keynes assumed that the time lags between initial expenditure and subsequent expenditure of incomes arising from that expenditure would not be 'unduly serious' [79: *343*], it is now generally appreciated that two or three years could pass before the full effects came through, during which time budget deficits might have had an adverse effect on financial confidence. T. Thomas [140], using a Keynesian model of the interwar economy, estimated the multiplier to be approximately 1.0 in the short run and 1.5 in the long run.[4] It should be added that Thomas's model is not designed to explain international capital flows, although a key element in the Treasury's case against Keynes was that, if public works seemed extravagant or wasteful, bondholders might prefer to take their money abroad, in the expectation that British government stock would fall in value [118: *173*].

Although it seems clear that Keynes exaggerated the employment-creating potential of public works, there continues to be a lively debate as to their possible contribution to a solution to unemployment. One school of thought argues that a high degree of regional specialisation in depressed industries such as coal and cotton, and a high propensity on the part of these regions to import consumer goods and building materials, would have militated against a Keynesian solution [11; 41; 44]. It is worth noting that Keynes himself admitted in 1937 that the stage of recovery then reached required a regional policy [84: *385*]. Howson [61] and Hatton [50], however, have pointed out that the distinction between, on the one hand, unemployment arising from a deficiency of aggregate demand and, on the other, unemployment of a structural or regional nature, is not absolute. When aggregate demand is high, workers are more encouraged to migrate and firms are more likely to invest in regions where labour is available. There is obviously much truth in this, but even at the best of times labour mobility in the interwar period was low [21: *190–221*] while new industrial development was overwhelmingly concentrated in the Greater London area [94: *101*].

It is nevertheless possible to argue, as Garside and Hatton [40] have done, that between 1920 and 1939 there was a deficiency of aggregate demand which could have been removed without an explosion of money incomes or prices. This case rests on the fact that throughout the period price changes were only partially reflected in wage rates. However, it is not certain that this would have continued to be so if unemployment had been reduced below the lowest levels of the interwar period (about 10 per cent of the insured labour force, or 8 per cent of the total workforce, in 1929 and 1937). Keynes himself in 1930 regarded 6½ per cent of the insured labour force as a 'normal' figure [72: 29]. All one can say is that the Keynesian case is stronger for periods of high cyclical unemployment, when prices were falling (1921–2; 1930–4) than for periods of cyclical recovery (1927–9; 1936–7), when prices were rising. In the latter periods, at least, macroeconomic policy would have been most effective if supplemented by measures to direct demand to areas or trades where there was suitable unemployed labour, and by microeconomic measures, such as industrial retraining, to improve the labour supply.

The experience of loan–financed rearmament in the later 1930s provides some indication of the problems which might have been encountered by a major public works programme earlier. The rearmament programme of 1936 led to additional defence expenditure totalling £440 million in the financial years 1936/37–1938/39, of which £193 million was financed by borrowing in 1937/38–1938/39. In scale this was broadly equivalent to what Lloyd George had asked for (additional loan–financed civil public capital expenditure of £250 million over two years). Defence expenditure was not, of course, strictly comparable to expenditure on public works, since armaments, unlike electrical transmission lines or roads, neither produced a money return nor reduced the costs of industrial production. On the other hand, even productive public works would have produced little direct financial return in two years. Moreover, the Ministry of Labour thought that rearmament was more likely to be helpful in reducing unemployment than public works were [115: 149]. Defence contracts affected a wider range of trades, and women could more easily be employed in factories than on roads or house–building. Mark Thomas [139] has calculated that rearmament created just over a million jobs between 1935 and 1938. This estimate must be regarded as a gross figure, since it takes no account of exports foregone when capacity was taken up with government contracts, but Mark Thomas's estimate for the multiplier, 1.6 in 1938, is not much above T. Thomas's estimate of about 1.5 [140]. Rearmament would certainly seem to have achieved all that Lloyd George hoped to do with his public works programme of 1929 – that is to create 611,000 jobs in two years. However, whereas Britain had had a balance-of-payments surplus on current account in 1935, prior to rearmament, the adverse balance by 1938 was such that Keynes and the Treasury could agree that the position was potentially no less serious than in 1931, when a crisis of confidence had led to a collapse in the sterling:dollar exchange rate [113: *96–9*; 115: *147–8*]. According to Kaldor (using an optimistic multiplier of 2) the position would have been even worse had an attempt been made to reduce unemployment in 1938 to 3 per cent of wage–earners, for then the balance-of-payments deficit on current account would have been such as to require either a 25 per cent increase in exports or a 15 per cent reduction in imports [8: *364–5*].

The experience of rearmament suggests that even productive loan-financed public works would not have achieved all that Keynes claimed. This does not, however, mean that Keynes was wrong to advocate them. A partial solution is better than no solution at all. All the same, the Treasury's insistence that public works should be economic, either in the sense of producing a money return comparable to commercial investment, or in the sense of lowering costs of production, would seem to have been justified. Greater competitiveness in international and home markets was essential if full employment were to be achieved without overwhelming balance-of-payments problems.

4   Towards a Managed Economy?

IN recent years a good deal of research has been done on two related questions: to what extent was there a movement towards a managed economy in the 1930s, and to what extent did any such movement reflect the influence of Keynes? It must be said that it is by no means easy to discover how economic ideas enter the policy-making process. Nevertheless, important work by Howson and Winch [63] and Middleton [104] has probably enabled us to learn more about the influence of economic ideas in the 1930s than about any other period. Even so, there remains the problem that many of the measures which Keynes advocated were also advocated by various pressure groups, albeit in less articulate ways. It is difficult to distinguish his influence from that of changes in public opinion – especially when he himself was an influence on informed public opinion [12]. What one can do is to compare the Treasury's ideas with those of Keynes, to see whether a convergence was taking place.

In a sense, Britain had been a managed economy since 1919, when, after the abandonment of the gold standard, changes in bank rate were for the first time made primarily to control domestic inflation rather than to preserve a fixed exchange rate. Likewise the return to the gold standard required monetary policy to be used to deflate the economy. The gold standard itself, however, acted as a major constraint on monetary policy. The Treasury regarded a reduction in bank rate as the principal means of countering a depression [118: *177–8*], and, as Howson's research has revealed, the Treasury since 1929 had wished to help business by lowering interest rates. Such a policy, however, was in conflict with one of maintaining a fixed exchange rate, which required that interest rates in London should be broadly in line with those in other financial centres. Once Britain had been forced off gold in September 1931, it was possible to give priority to domestic monetary policy [20: *35–52, 99–103*; 58: *68, 86*; 106].

Howson [58: *85–6, 143*] has identified Phillips, who was Hopkins's immediate subordinate on the financial side of the Treasury, as an important source of new ideas about this time. As wholesale prices fell in the post–1929 depression, but wage–costs remained comparatively rigid, businessmen were discouraged by falling profits and they laid off workers. In 1932 Phillips advocated the remedy of raising wholesale prices to at least 25 per cent above the level of September 1931, while helping exporters, by allowing sterling to depreciate. A rise in prices would also reduce the real burden of the National Debt, the interest on which was the largest item in the budget. The Treasury's choice of policy instruments, however, was designed to maintain financial confidence. The orthodoxy of balanced budgets was maintained, so that City opinion would accept a reduction in interest rates on government stock. Bank rate fell from 6 per cent to 2 per cent in 1932, and stayed at that level, apart from a brief rise at the outbreak of war, until 1951. Restrictions were placed on overseas investment, and it was hoped that economic recovery would come about through private enterprise. Public works were at first abandoned, and were reintroduced in the later 1930s only on a modest scale [119: *92–110*]. The Treasury's response to the Macmillan Report's call for more conscious and deliberate management in financial policy could thus fairly be described as conservative (except for the Exchange Equalisation Account – see Chapter 2). This was true even of domestic monetary policy, for while cheap money was certainly intended to encourage private investment, this was not the Treasury's first priority. The Treasury was still concerned about the size of the National Debt, and the balance between short and long–term Debt. This led the Treasury to take advantage of low interest rates to convert Treasury bills into long–term issues, although it was aware of the argument that this could be deflationary: since banks used Treasury bills as secondary reserves, a reduction in their holdings would tend to restrict bank lending [58: *90, 95–104, 133–5*].

It is difficult to summarise Keynes's own policy suggestions in the 1930s, for his fertile mind seized on many ideas. Indeed, there was a malicious saying that, where five economists were gathered together, there would be six opinions and that two of them would be put forward by Keynes [16: *90*]. In fact Keynes had presented the Macmillan Committee with a menu of no less than seven policy options in 1930 [12: *170–77*; 25; 83: *38–157*]. The first option was devaluation, which Keynes did not favour until other expedients had been tried, since it would disturb international credit. It was only after the Report was signed in 1931 that he realised that devaluation was inevitable. As we have seen (Chapter 2) the Treasury did adopt Keynes's idea of a managed exchange rate, once Britain had been forced off gold in September 1931. Keynes's second option in 1930 was an agreed reduction in all domestic money incomes, but he felt that this would face too many practical difficulties. In the event, the Treasury's policy from 1932 of raising prices had the effect of reducing real incomes without the necessity for a formal agreement, something which Keynes certainly favoured. Keynes's third option in 1930 was to subsidise certain industries, but he did not press this proposal. His fourth option was rationalisation of industry, but he doubted whether it was practicable to increase efficiency sufficiently to restore equilibrium. His fifth option was protection, which would reduce real wages as well as reduce imports, but again he did not think that protection would be adequate to the situation. Later, in 1931, he was to advocate a revenue tariff, but then took the view that currency depreciation in 1931–2 made tariffs unnecessary. Although Keynes wrote in 1933 in favour of greater self–sufficiency, the general tariff introduced in 1932 owed nothing to his influence [74: 10–21] and he always regarded protection as a second–best policy for influencing employment [35].

Keynes did not reject any of the first five proposals – indeed he said later that he favoured an eclectic programme, using all remedies which tended in the right direction [83: 375]. Nevertheless, he made clear to the Macmillan Committee that his sixth option – a reduction in savings by increasing expenditure on home-produced goods – was his favourite. This could be done by increasing current consumption, but he noted that from a long–term point of view this would be less beneficial than creating capital assets, for it was through the latter that the wealth of the nation was increased. Everything should be done to encourage private investment, but Keynes believed that business confidence was at such a low ebb that it would be necessary for the government to break the vicious circle with investment which would restore business profits. However, as we have seen in Chapter 3, Keynes's arguments in favour of public works carried little weight with the Treasury at this time.

Keynes's seventh option was for international action by central banks to raise world prices to the level of money incomes and money costs of production, so as to cut business losses. However, as already noted in Chapter 2, international co–operation was at a low ebb in the early 1930s.

This brief survey of Keynes's views in 1930 suggests that it is easy both to oversimplify his ideas and to exaggerate his influence on policy in the slump. The case for Keynes having an influence on the Treasury has been made out most strongly by Howson and Winch [63] in relation to the later 1930s. The Economic Advisory Council's Committee on Economic Information, of which Keynes was the leading member, was joined by Phillips in 1935, and Howson has suggested that by the later 1930s the arguments used by Phillips and Hopkins, on such matters as cheap money and counter–cyclical public works, reflected a belief that government ought to assume some responsibility for maintaining aggregate demand [58: *143*]. Undoubtedly Treasury officials must have been made more aware of the theoretical issues as they took part in discussions with economists. However, there are reasons for believing that no 'Keynesian revolution' had taken place in policy by 1939.

While it would be difficult, given the profusion of ideas that poured from Keynes's mind, to define just what such a revolution would have amounted to, one can identify four critical issues in domestic economic policy in the period 1932–9, when the Treasury was managing the exchange rate broadly to Keynes's satisfaction. These issues are the respective attitudes of Keynes and the Treasury to public works, domestic monetary policy, fiscal policy, and macroeconomic theory. As regards public works, we have seen that Keynes was consistently more optimistic than the Treasury as regards the effects of loan–expenditure on employment. The Treasury believed in 1939, as it had done in 1929, that the real stimulus from such expenditure came from reflationary finance, without which public works would merely replace private investment [114: *6*]. On the other hand, by 1937 the Treasury was worried about the slump which would result from the simultaneous exhaustion of the housing boom and the end of the rearmament programme, about 1941. In consequence, the Treasury agreed to advance planning of public works [58: *127–30*; 63: *140–3*; 104: *168–70*]. However, as noted in Chapter 3, what was envisaged was a modest variation in normal annual capital expenditure, not a large–scale programme for additional public works. Moreover, Phillips made plain that a reduction of interest rates would continue to be the principal means of combating a depression [118: *177–8*].

This might seem a surprising conclusion, given that bank rate was as low as 2 per cent in 1937, compared with 5 to 6.5 per cent at the previous cyclical peak (1929). However, loan–financed rearmament was getting into its stride in 1937 and the Treasury anticipated that a rise in bank rate to 4 per cent or more would be necessary to prevent a rearmament-led boom getting out of hand [58: *129–31*]. Keynes, on the other hand, following his *General Theory*, was an advocate of low, stable interest rates in a boom as well as a slump, for if financial markets came to expect higher interest rates, it would be difficult to reverse the trend. Low interest rates would enable the boom to last and the correct policy for the Treasury was to control demand through taxation [78: *320–2*; 84: *388–91*;109:*234–42*].

Fiscal policy had received only a passing mention in the *General Theory* [78: *95*]. However, it should not be inferred from this that Keynes regarded it as unimportant. Keynes conceded that balanced budgets created confidence in financial circles and thereby tended to lower the long-term rate of interest. However, he also argued that the balanced-budget rule could be suspended in a slump, on the grounds that excess spending would raise demand, and thereby national income, so that after a short delay increased revenue would enable the chancellor to balance his budget again. Treasury officials, on the other hand, while conceding that unbalanced budgets did not lead immediately to inflation, argued that once the principle that the budget should always be balanced had been abandoned, it would be impossible politically to restrain demand for higher expenditure, even in a boom [102: *53–61*]. The Treasury regarded unbalanced budgets to pay for rearmament as an unpleasant necessity, akin to a wartime emergency, and thought that it would be unfortunate if the country began to think of a defence loan as a 'comfortable Lloyd-Georgian device' [58: *123*; 113: *74*]. Indeed, Hopkins thought that, in order to preserve the government's financial reputation, there would have to be increased debt redemption after 1941, despite the anticipated slump [114: *9*].

It is possible to argue that further evidence of the pre–Keynesian nature of the Treasury in the later 1930s may be found in its attitude to the macroeconomic approach of the *General Theory*. The

Treasury made no attempt to compile national income statistics, although the Inland Revenue had shown in 1929 that this could be done. As we shall see, the Treasury was to use Keynes's macroeconomic approach in preparing its wartime budgets from 1941, but in 1937 the Treasury related its borrowing programme to vague estimates of the current level of savings, without working out how these might be affected by changes in national income [113: *75–9*; 114: *7–9*]. On the other hand, as Patinkin [111] has pointed out, Keynes himself failed to exert his influence in Whitehall to get official national income studies underway before 1940. Moreover, the Treasury was moving towards macroeconomic management through fiscal policy. As Middleton [104: *118–21*] has shown, by 1939 the Treasury was using the balance between government borrowing and revenue to allow aggregate demand to rise.

Even so, reviewing the Treasury's attitude to public works, domestic monetary policy, fiscal policy and macroeconomic theory, it is difficult to avoid the conclusion that Britain was still some way from being a managed economy on Keynesian lines in 1939. This impression is reinforced if one looks at the Treasury's attitudes to proposals in 1942–4 for post–war employment policy (see Chapter 6). First, however, it is best to look at how national income accounting was adopted by the Treasury for the purpose of war finance.

5 How to Pay for the War

MACROECONOMIC management, based on a national accounting analytical framework, was introduced in Britain with the 1941 budget. This budget was described by Keynes as 'a revolution in public finance' [85: *353–4*] in that, together with an accompanying White Paper on national income and expenditure, it dealt with aggregate demand and supply, and was no longer simply a cash balance sheet of central government income and expenditure. However, it was a revolution brought about by the problem of inflation, not unemployment. Government's war expenditure had taken up the slack in the economy by late 1940, and at full employment the differences between Keynes and pre-Keynesian economists disappeared [78: *378–9*]. It is not really surprising therefore that, as Tomlinson [142: *131–2*] has noted, pre-war critics of Keynes such as Hayek, should agree with him on the economics of scarcity. Moreover, the balance-of-payments problem was removed for the duration of the war by the willingness of the United States, from 1941, to supply essential goods under Lend Lease. Thus there is reason to doubt Feinstein's claim [37: *12–13*] that the 1941 budget was the first to show acceptance of Keynes's theories and that 'it was but a short step' from wartime budgetary policy to the government's acceptance in 1944 of a commitment to maintain high and stable employment after the war.

In 1941 aggregate demand was excessive, and the Treasury was willing to use national income accounting to calculate by how much consumer demand must be reduced in order to avoid inflation. This was quite a different matter from agreeing that unemployment could be cured by raising domestic aggregate demand, especially in a post-war world when the balance of payments would once more be a constraint. The 1941 'revolution in public finance' and the 'Keynesian revolution' in employment policy thus deserve to be treated as separate issues.

The Treasury's attitude to war finance in 1939–40 has been characterised by Pollard [122: *212*] as 'timid', on the grounds that only half of the proposed expenditure was to be raised by taxation. This judgement reflects contemporary criticisms by Keynes who, in his pamphlet *How to Pay for the War* [79: *367–439*], said that the Treasury should no longer rely on its traditional method of assessing what the taxpayer would bear, and then borrowing the sums required over and above this figure. Instead, Keynes argued, the Treasury should calculate the national income, then work out how to transfer to the government that part of the national income which was needed to wage the war without inflation. The aim of war finance should be to reduce the amount of money in the hands of the public so that prices would not rise, even although total earnings were greater and the supply of consumer goods was less than before the war. Keynes predicted that voluntary savings would be inadequate for the sums which the government wished to borrow, and he estimated that there was an inflationary 'gap' which could only be filled by increased taxation or by a rise in prices. The latter would increase money incomes, so that the public would be able to subscribe to a greatly increased National Debt, while still attempting to buy more goods than could be bought at current prices. Keynes's fiscal proposals were designed to reduce money incomes during the war, while promising to make partial repayments after the war. Keynes thought that, if 'deferred pay' were released at the onset of a post-war slump, it would be possible to maintain aggregate demand without resort to loan-financed public works. In his view, this would make his scheme for deferred pay self-liquidating both in terms of finance and of real resources, for the extra post-war consumption would be met out of labour and productive capacity which would otherwise have been idle.

It is easy to criticise the Treasury for being conservative, as Pollard does, in its distrust of Keynes's calculations. However, some points may be made on the other side. In the first place, Treasury officials were aware that the problem of war finance was not simply a problem of inventing ingenious monetary devices. It was also a question of the feelings of the working population, [5] and the fact was that the trade unions were opposed to reductions in working-class living standards, even although Keynes had linked his scheme for deferred pay with further schemes for family allowances and price controls on basic rations. Moreover, even talk of compulsory savings was apparently enough to reduce the flow of voluntary savings into the National Savings movement. In the end, the prospect of defeat in 1940 made public opinion more inclined to accept draconian measures and in 1941 the standard rate of income tax was raised to 10s. in the pound compared with 5s.6d. before the war. The 1941 budget also saw the introduction of Keynes's scheme for deferred pay, or what came to be called post-war credits, but the scheme never achieved the importance which Keynes had suggested. On average, only £121 million a year was raised through it, whereas Keynes had mentioned an annual figure of £550 million [130: 33–5, 80–5]. Moreover, Keynes's belief that post-war credits would be self–liquidating proved to be illusory, since the post-war slump which he anticipated did not materialise. In the event, personal post-war credits had to be peddled out slowly, and in greatly depreciated currency, to old–age pensioners and other special cases.

Keynes's major contribution to war finance was the logical structure of the 1941 budget and White Paper. The national accounting framework drew on the pioneering work of Colin Clark and Erwin Rothbarth [29], and work on official national income statistics by James Meade and Richard Stone enjoyed the support of Hopkins [85: 325–8]. The national income accounts presented in 1941 were necessarily less than perfect and could give the Treasury only an approximation as to the magnitude of the inflationary gap. Moreover, money national income was increasing rapidly in the first half of the war (by a total of about 36 per cent between 1940 and 1943) so that statistics tended to lag behind reality, while there were further lags in the adjustment of taxation in annual budgets. [6] Nevertheless, war finance in 1941–5 was a considerable improvement on that of 1914–18, when the government had relied heavily upon inflationary borrowing. It should be noted, however, that inflation was contained in 1941–5, not only by fiscal means but also by financial and physical controls over investment which suppressed alternatives to the purchase of government bonds. Moreover, wage restraint was encouraged by a policy of price controls and food subsidies, with rationing to ensure 'fair shares for all'.

The Treasury and the Bank of England agreed with Keynes that high interest rates should not be offered on government bonds, as this would raise the burden of the National Debt, as had happened in the First World War. However, few people would lend to the government for more than short periods at low interest rates, with the result that the public emerged from the war with accumulated purchasing power in the form of cash balances or short-term assets. Keynes was aware of this problem, but he did not anticipate that inflationary pressure would persist beyond five years after the war, and he expected that a prolongation of direct controls and rationing would be able to deal with the problem. This would allow interest rates to be kept low, ready for a post-war slump [149: 44–5, 52–3].

Keynes's ideas on fiscal and monetary policy worked well enough during the war, but clearly circumstances were exceptional. This helps to explain why Treasury officials did not see that there 'was but a short step' from acceptance of Keynes's ideas on how to pay for the war to acceptance of a commitment to maintain high and stable employment after the war.

6 The 1944 White Paper on Employment Policy

'THE Government accept as one of their primary aims and responsibilities the maintenance of a high and stable level of employment after the war.' This commitment in the 1944 White Paper on *Employment Policy* has generally been recognised as a major change in policy priorities. On the other hand, it is also true that the White Paper incorporated compromises between traditional ideas and the theories of Keynes and his followers [1: *242–7*; 10; 46; 116; 142: *132–4*; 145: *15–33*; 149: *48–67*; 150: *269–73*]. The White Paper outlined a threefold approach to employment policy. Firstly, in collaboration with other countries, efforts were being made to create favourable international conditions in which exports could expand (see Chapter 2). Secondly, with emphasis on the transition from a war economy, there were to be microeconomic measures to prevent unemployment arising from a maldistribution of industry and labour. Thirdly, with reference to the period after the transition, there were to be macroeconomic measures to maintain aggregate demand. Keynes was personally involved as the Treasury's representative in negotiations with the United States on what became the Bretton Woods agreements on stable exchange rates and the establishment of the International Monetary Fund. He was also, of course, deeply interested in macroeconomic policy, in his capacity as an economic adviser within the Treasury. In general, however, he was much less interested in microeconomic policy. Indeed the White Paper's chapters dealing with the location of industry and the adaptability of labour owed nothing to Keynes's economic theory, but had their origins respectively in the Board of Trade and the Ministry of Labour [9; 46: *156–7*]. The discussion which follows is necessarily centred on Keynes and the Treasury, but the diversity of influences on the White Paper is recognised. The questions considered here are: firstly, to what extent was the commitment to maintain high and stable employment the result of Keynes's influence? Secondly, to what extent did the *means* by which it was proposed to achieve that objective represent acceptance by the Treasury of Keynes's ideas?

The commitment to maintain high and stable employment was, of course, partly the product of the politics of war. The experience of mass unemployment in the interwar years had not in itself been enough to put employment policy to the fore in the 1930s, perhaps because the unemployed had been a minority of the electorate, even when unemployment had been at its highest. In wartime, however, so many people were in the forces or were employed in munitions production, that it was quite likely that a large proportion of the electorate feared that they might be among the unlucky ones in a post–war slump. Moreover, the experience of full employment during the war may have contributed to a popular belief that governments could solve unemployment, even although the war economy had been sustained only with the help of American Lend Lease, which would not be available after the war. The experience of war, however, did not necessarily lead to acceptance of Keynes's macroeconomic analysis. The physical allocation of productive resources, as in the war economy, was a widely canvassed alternative, and some Labour members of the Coalition Government took the view that slumps could be controlled only if such government powers were extended [19: 299–318]. The Beveridge Report of 1942 was founded on the assumption that 'full employment' could be maintained, but at that date Sir William Beveridge believed that this could be achieved through a continuation of wartime planning, and it was not until later that he was converted to the Keynesianism of his *Full Employment in a Free Society* of 1944 [47: 428–34].

On the other hand, it is possible, as *The Times* believed in 1944, that the government was able to accept responsibility for employment because the work of economists influenced by Keynes, and the accumulation of statistical knowledge, had 'laid bare the essential mechanism of the national economy'.[7] Certainly the 'Keynesian revolution' in economic thought had made its mark on economists who had been recruited as temporary civil servants in the War Cabinet secretariat. From 1941 Lionel Robbins, the head of the Economic Section, with James Meade and others, pressed for macroeconomic policies to maintain a high and stable demand for labour [10: 107–11; 116: 286–8; 126: 150–2, 186–9]. Moreover, Keynes himself was a persuasive advocate of his ideas, once he was in close, continuous contact with Treasury officials. On questions such as the practicality of the techniques of macroeconomic management, ministers were highly dependent upon their advisers, and here Treasury officials played a crucial role. Hopkins was chairman of an official interdepartmental Steering Committee on Post-War Employment, the report [8] of which formed the basis of the 1944 White Paper. It is therefore best to pass on to the question, 'to what extent did the policies outlined in the White Paper represent acceptance by the Treasury of Keynes's ideas?' before forming a view as to the extent of Keynes's influence on the government's commitment to maintain high and stable employment.

On the fundamental importance of Britain's post-war balance of payments there was no disagreement between Keynes and Treasury officials. Loss of overseas investments meant that Britain would have to export more in order to pay for her pre-war level of imports. Moreover, given Britain's dependence upon imported food, raw materials and, in the period of post-war reconstruction, capital equipment, a much reduced level of imports would imply a lower level of economic activity and, therefore, of employment. Since Britain was unlikely to increase her share of world exports in the long run, she could best hope to increase the volume of her exports if the volume of world trade increased [24: *96–125*]. The Americans too were interested in non–discriminatory, multilaterial trade, but Henderson who, like Keynes, was an economic adviser in the Treasury, warned that Britain's balance of payments would be so desperate after the war that she would have to adopt more restrictive commercial policies than the United States would like [55: *209–19*]. Keynes himself was uncertain whether the negotiations with the Americans would have a satisfactory outcome. Uncertainty about the future of the export trades and the balance of payments helps to explain some of the scepticism with which proposals for reducing unemployment by raising aggregate demand were met by some senior Treasury officials, principally Sir Wilfrid Eady [10: *103*]. In the end the White Paper warned that if demand for important exports fell, it would be necessary to find alternative exports. Keynes accepted that domestic policy could not offset completely a loss of external markets, but he thought that the seriousness of Britain's post-war balance of payments would be a reason why the primary impulse to unemployment simply could not be allowed to come from a loss of exports [116: *290–1*].

Keynes himself expected that the domestic problems of the post-war period would come in three stages. Firstly, there would be temporary inflationary pressure, as in 1919–20, but physical controls over investment would make it possible to hold interest rates low. Secondly, after about five years, there would follow a period of cyclical instability, with no marked trend towards chronic deflation. Thirdly, such a trend would become evident, ten to twenty years ahead, unless prevented by appropriate policies. It was because of this anticipated third stage that he was anxious not to allow interest rates to rise in the first two stages, for he believed that once people had become accustomed to higher interest rates it would be difficult to revert to a cheap money policy [149: 50–3]. The White Paper, however, dealt only with the first two of Keynes's stages, and confined its macroeconomic proposals largely to contra-cyclical public investment, with only tentative ideas as to how private investment or expenditure on consumers' goods might be influenced.

The White Paper endorsed Keynes's view that monetary policy alone would not be sufficient to stabilise private investment (especially in a depression), but it was ambiguous about future variations in interest rates, while alternative means of influencing investment, such as tax credits, were only hinted at. Likewise there was a scheme (never implemented) for varying social insurance contributions according to the level of unemployment, 'when settled conditions return', and, even more tentatively, the possibility was held out of budget surpluses in good years and tax credits in bad years. The White Paper was also ambiguous about deficit finance: it was stated that there was to be no deliberate planning for deficits in the central government's budget, although there was nothing to prevent the chancellor from taking into account the requirements of trade and employment when framing his budget [36: 20–5]. There was some justice in Beveridge's criticism that the White Paper was really a public works policy, aimed at mitigating fluctuations in the level of demand, rather than a programme for a steady expansion of demand [8: 261–3, 270–4].

Treasury officials were largely responsible for the conservative tone of the White Paper. [9] This was true even of Hopkins, who was more inclined than his colleagues to be sympathetic to Keynes's ideas [63: 108–9, 152; 116]. There is some doubt, however, as to Keynes's own attitude to the White Paper. Wilson [149: 48–9, 55–8], using the evidence of Keynes's own writings, has argued that Keynes himself favoured balanced budgets for central government's current expenditure. Both public investment programmes (largely in the hands of local authorities or public corporations, like the Central Electricity Board) and variations in social insurance contributions should, in Keynes's view, be in a separate capital budget. On the other hand, Booth [10: *106, 114-6*] has shown that Keynes was ambivalent about budget orthodoxy, at least to the extent of being prepared to contemplate deficit finance for current expenditure, once the demand for capital was much more saturated than it was in the 1940s. Hopkins argued successfully against a capital budget, on the grounds that politicians would be tempted to transfer to it expenditure of a non-self-liquidating character, which ought to be met out of revenue. He also rejected the principle that budget deficits could be justified by the existence of unemployment, and instead interpolated into the White Paper the idea of varying the size of the budget surplus [116: *292-3*]. Whatever Keynes's position on budget orthodoxy, it seems plain that the Treasury had not been wholly converted to his ideas by 1944. This, together with the fact that the Board of Trade's and the Ministry of Labour's important contributions were made without reference to Keynes, suggests that Keynes's influence on the government's commitment to full employment was more limited than has been suggested by some writers, for example Feinstein [37: *13*] and Stewart [137: *185-6*].

How justified was the Treasury's scepticism? There is room here to touch on only three issues: stability of prices and wages; mobility of labour, and estimates of the multiplier. Keynes's employment policy depended for its success upon his assumption in the *General Theory* that, while workers would usually resist money wage cuts, reductions in real wages would not be resisted 'unless they proceeded to an extreme degree' [78: *14*]. Even economists who had adopted Keynes's analysis, such as Meade, were inclined to think that real-wage resistance would be greater than Keynes had supposed in 1936 [69: *12, 20-32*]. Keynes did not oppose Meade's suggestion in 1943 that a moderate wages policy would be necessary in order to prevent a vicious spiral of rising wages and prices in conditions of full employment, but in the event the proposal was dropped because the Ministry of Labour anticipated trade union opposition to interference with free collective bargaining [10: *111-12, 114*]. Keynes himself confessed in 1945 that he knew of no solution to the wages problem [89: *385*]. The White Paper did indeed warn that stability of prices and wages was a condition of success for employment policy [36: *18-19*]. However, in Britain, at least, such stability has proved to be elusive, with the consequence that much of the multiplier effect of expenditure has been lost in higher prices.

The Treasury was sceptical of the Economic Section's assumption of sufficient labour mobility to prevent structural unemployment [116: *287, 291*]. Once more the White Paper contained a highly pertinent warning: if workers failed to move to places and occupations where they were needed, then an attempt to cure unemployment by raising aggregate demand could lead to a dangerous rise in prices [36: *20*]. Subsequent experience does not suggest that the Treasury was wrong to draw attention to the importance of microeconomic aspects of the labour market.

Moreover, Keynes, even in 1944, was far too optimistic in regard to the multiplier, which he thought would be approximately 2 for public investment and 3 for reductions in social insurance contributions [10: *113*]. Wilson [149: *56–8*] regards the latter figure as particularly odd, given Keynes's belief that people's consumer expenditure would not be much influenced by short–term changes in income and, in Wilson's opinion, Keynes had simply got himself into a muddle. Presumably what Keynes had in mind was that national insurance contributors, the majority of whom were working class, would be less likely to save additional income than people paying income tax, the majority of whom were middle class. Be that as it may, Henderson's belief in 1944 that the multiplier effect of variations in social insurance contributions would be subject to indeterminate time–lags [55: *322–3*] seems to have carried weight with Treasury officials and the White Paper contained no explicit reference to the multiplier, let alone any estimates.

7   A 'Keynesian Revolution'?

ARGUMENTS about whether or when a 'Keynesian revolution' took place in British economic policy in the 1940s have been bedevilled by lack of a clear definition of what such a revolution would imply. Winch [150: *281–3*] was content to state that the Keynesian revolution was not limited to employment policy, but was best thought of 'as a rational approach to the problems of economic management in general', including price stability. Such a definition is too broad, however, unless it be conceded that Keynesian economists have a monopoly of rationality. The word 'Keynesian' itself has acquired too broad a meaning to be unambiguous, since it is applied to ideas of Keynes's followers, and there has been lively debate about whether Keynes himself would have agreed with these ideas [64]. What follows is based upon the views of Keynes rather than those of his followers.

The 1944 White Paper on *Employment Policy* had not committed the government to any particular level of 'high and stable employment'. However, Keynes's own target for post-war unemployment was higher than what became the maximum which was politically acceptable, and what was experienced, down to 1975. In 1942, Keynes suggested a 'standard' figure of 5 per cent, if there were no deficiency in aggregate demand, and in 1944 he commented on Beveridge's target of 3 per cent that there was no harm in trying, but that he did not expect it to be achieved [72: *29–30*; 149: *59*]. In 1951, however, the Labour government stated that 3 per cent was the maximum level of unemployment which would be tolerated [46: *159*]. Thereafter, all governments appeared to conduct fiscal and monetary policy as if this were so, until inflation became an even more pressing political problem in the mid–1970s. Keynes had thought that it would be possible to manage demand so that there would be full employment without inflation [149: *42*] and there is no way of knowing what his advice would have been in a period of stagflation. The fact that from the mid–1970s politicians gave a higher priority to the problem of inflation is not evidence that they had not been true converts to Keynesianism earlier. With regard to the use of Keynes's macroeconomic concepts, Hugh Dalton, Labour's first post–war chancellor, had Keynes as an adviser until the latter's death in April 1946. Moreover Meade, who succeeded Robbins as director of the Economic Section in 1945, was admitted to the Treasury's Budget Committee.Even so, Dalton's first budgets have been seen as retrograde so far as the use of national income accounting methods were concerned [150: 283]. Little was heard, at least in public, of Keynes's concept of the 'inflationary gap', which had featured so prominently in wartime budgets (see Chapter 5). It was only with the weakening of controls inherited from the war that Keynesian techniques came gradually to the fore. From Dalton's budget of November 1947 onwards analysis of the 'inflationary gap' was once again a major constituent of budgetary policy [19: 409–26; 31; 120: 452–3, 468–75].

The impact of Keynesian economics on Treasury thinking in this period is a controversial subject. Booth [10: 118, 122–3] has contrasted the lack of economic literacy among top Treasury officials down to 1947 with their apparent skill in macroeconomics shortly thereafter, and he has concluded that it was the inflationary pressure of that year which converted the Treasury to Keynesianism. Tomlinson [144] has argued that such a conversion did not amount to a 'Keynesian revolution' in policy-making, for which the crucial test was unemployment, not price stability, and he has reiterated the view that there never was a 'Keynesian revolution', since sound finance has never been subordinated to employment policy [141; 142; 143]. In Tomlinson's view, the key factor was the private financial system's reluctance to fund public sector deficits. However, it is surely the case that, as Tomlinson himself admits [145: 102–4], there are other important elements in a 'Keynesian revolution' apart from private sector finance for budget deficits. As we have seen, Keynes was ambivalent towards budget deficits, but he did prefer investment in capital assets to deficits on current account. Moreover, within limits, it was possible in the post-war period to manage the economy in a Keynesian fashion even when the budget was in surplus. The size of the surplus could be varied, and tax changes used to influence aggregate demand [31: 198–200]. Indeed tax changes rather than variations in public investment became the normal means of managing demand.

Rollings [127] has criticised Booth's conclusions from the perspective of one who is familiar with the relevant Treasury records in the immediate post-war period. Rollings has shown that practical considerations rather than economic doctrines explain the Treasury's shift in 1947 from the idea of a balanced budget to the idea of a budget surplus to counter inflation. Physical controls over the economy were weakening and fiscal policy afforded the Treasury the opportunity to reassert its traditional control over public expenditure. Fiscal policy also helped to restore the Treasury to its position as the central department of government. The Treasury could thus readily embrace the idea of a budget surplus even although leading officials were sceptical of forecasts provided by Meade of the inflationary gap between national income and expenditure. Indeed, Keynes himself shared official scepticism of forecasts in 1945–6, and said that the margin of error was too great to permit fine tuning [19: 413–14].

Further research is needed into the Treasury's records in order to discover whether or when the Treasury became 'Keynesian'. The fact that the economy was a full employment for so long after 1945 makes it difficult to draw conclusions from policy and from public statements alone. For example, Sir Leslie Rowan, one of the leading Treasury officials dealing with economic policy from 1947 to 1958, warned that the 'creeping inflation' of the 1950s (averaging less than 5 per cent a year) would discourage savings and reduce the funds available for investment [129: 22–5]. Such a view could have come from the era of pre–Keynesian economics, but then Keynes had said that the classical economists had been right in believing that savings were necessary for investment when the economy was at full employment [78: 372–3]. It follows that Treasury concern about prices and savings in the post-war period cannot be dismissed as pre-Keynesian.

As regards monetary policy, the continuation of a cheap money policy after the war conformed to Keynes's advice. He believed that the long-term rate of interest was determined by expectations of what future interest rates were likely to be, as well as by the maturity composition of people's portfolios, and that therefore nothing should be done to raise interest rates when the economy was at full employment, lest this make it impossible to reduce them in a slump. Moreover, it is known that Hopkins made use of Keynes's ideas when advising the chancellor in 1945 on National Debt policy [116: 294], Hopkins's memorandum being liberally laced with quotations from the *General Theory*. However, there were plenty of practical reasons for avoiding a repetition of the high interest rates which had occurred after the First World War. Low interest rates kept down the cost of borrowing, at a time when large-scale housing and nationalisation programmes had to be financed. Moreover physical controls made it possible, at least in principle, to allocate capital resources, even in the private sector, without reliance upon bank rate. Paradoxically, the 'Keynesian' Meade favoured a return to a free domestic capital market, even if this meant high interest rates, for he believed that the price mechanism was more efficient than physical controls [97: 26–33, 83–5].

The 'Keynesian Revolution' in economic policy, like most, if not all, revolutions, was incomplete. One may draw some tentative conclusions from the five areas identified in Chapter 1 as being aspects of Treasury policy capable of being modified by Keynes's ideas. These were: international monetary policy, domestic monetary policy, public investment as an employment policy, use of macroeconomic concepts and fiscal policy. As noted in Chapter 2, Keynes himself was largely responsible for international monetary policy as embodied in the Bretton Woods agreements, but these represented what could be negotiated with the Americans rather than what Keynes regarded as desirable in the best of all possible worlds. One might well surmise that Keynes would have regarded British exchange-rate policy between the devaluations of 1949 and 1967 as too inflexible – certainly commitment to a stable exchange rate in these years involved fiscal and monetary measures to hold back demand whenever the exchange rate was threatened [31]. On the other hand, there was in that period no attempt to *raise* the sterling:dollar exchange rate, as in 1919–25. As regards domestic monetary policy, this seemed to follow Keynes's advice so long as there were other controls on investment, but Keynes's stress on stable interest rates would seem to have had a diminishing influence on policy in the period after 1951, when the Conservative government reverted to the pre–1932 practice of making active use of changes in bank rate to control the level of investment. With regard to public investment as an employment policy, Rollings's research has revealed evidence that the Treasury showed some willingness to adopt Keynes's ideas in 1945–7, by taking steps to enable such a policy to be implemented quickly [127: 96–7]. In the event, of course, these projects were not required for that purpose in the long post-war boom. Keynes's macroeconomic concepts had been introduced into Treasury thought in 1940/41 and from November 1947 fiscal policy was used actively to deflate demand. However, independent research by Cairncross and Rollings (unpublished at the time of writing) has provided evidence to suggest that as late as 1954/55 the chancellor and senior Treasury officials had not been converted to the idea of budget deficits to stimulate demand. It is difficult to trace the influence of economic theory on policy even when the public records are available and, at the time of writing, only the records for the first ten post-war years are available under the 30 Year Rule. Moreover, the sheer mass of records makes it difficult for researchers to absorb them, and there is inevitably a lag between research and publication. One may note, however, that it is possible to explain the growing emphasis on demand management from the late 1940s by reference to the decline of other ways of controlling the economy, and also to the Treasury's wish to re-establish its position in Whitehall.

As for the historical significance of the adoption of Keynesian demand management techniques, it should be noted that these alone have proved to be inadequate to ensure full employment, and that microeconomic measures to improve the efficiency of the supply side of the economy have been found to be necessary [4]. It does not follow from this that Keynes was wrong to emphasise the importance of macroeconomic factors, but post–war experience suggests that the Treasury's insistence in referring to microeconomic problems should not be dismissed as mere nit–picking. Moreover, public expenditure has given rise to powerful pressure groups in favour of particular forms of public expenditure, and politicians have found it hard to curb such pressures, in the absence of the old orthodox rules of public finance, even when unemployment was low [17]. When high levels of unemployment did recur in the 1970s and 1980s, inflationary circumstances made it difficult to apply Keynes's prescriptions of 40 years earlier. Keynes recognised that economics, unlike the typical natural science, deals with material which is not homogeneous through time [107: 55]. The experience of stagflation suggests that economics is akin to medical science, where the attempt to solve a problem may change its nature, as when, for example, a virus develops an immunity to a drug, and a new treatment has to be developed. However, if this is a useful analogy, it also suggests that one cannot disprove Keynes's case simply by referring to the apparent failure of Keynesian policies in the 1970s. The post–1929 depression was marked by falling prices, and cheap imports of raw materials ensured that depreciation of the sterling exchange rate in 1931–2 did not have inflationary consequences. The extent to which Keynes's methods would have reduced unemployment in the depression is debatable, but the consequences would not have been the same as in the 1970s, when prices in general were rising and when OPEC in particular was able to force up oil prices. The arguments of both Keynes and the Treasury embodied some wisdom, and the ideal 'Keynesian revolution' in policy might have been one which incorporated the best of both.

APPENDIX: Dramatis Personae

Beveridge, Sir William : author of Beveridge Report on *Social Insurance and Allied Services* (1942), and of *Full Employment in a Free Society* (1944).

Bradbury, Sir John : Joint Permanent Secretary, Treasury, 1913–19. Member of Cunliffe Committee, Committee on Currency and Bank of England Note Issues and Macmillan Committee.

Bridges, Sir Edward : Treasury official 1919–38. Cabinet Secretary 1938–46. Permanent Secretary, Treasury, 1945–56.

Chamberlain, Sir Austen : Chancellor of the Exchequer 1919–21. Chairman of Committee on the Currency and Bank of England Note Issues.

Chamberlain, Neville : Chancellor of the Exchequer 1923–4, 1931–7, Prime Minister 1937–40.

Churchill, Winston : Chancellor of the Exchequer 1924–9. Prime Minister 1940–5.

Clark, Colin : on staff of Economic Advisory Council 1930–1; lecturer in Statistics, Cambridge, 1931–7.

Dalton, Hugh : Chancellor of the Exchequer 1945–7.

Eady, Sir Wilfrid : Joint Second Secretary, Treasury, 1942–52.

Fisher, Sir Warren : Permanent Secretary, Treasury, 1919–39.

Grigg, P.J. : Principal Private Secretary to successive Chancellors of the Exchequer 1921–30.

Hawtrey, Ralph : Director of Financial Enquiries, Treasury, 1919–45. Hawtrey was the Treasury's sole economist between the wars.

Hayek, F.A. von : Professor of Economic Science and Statistics, University of London 1931–50.

Henderson, Hubert : Economist, co–author with Keynes of *Can Lloyd George Do It?* (1929). Joint Secretary, Economic Advisory Council 1930–9. Economic Adviser, Treasury, 1939–44.

Hopkins, Sir Richard : Controller of Finance and Supply Services 1927–32; Second Secretary 1932–42; Permanent Secretary 1942–5.

Jewkes, John : Professor of Social Economics, University of Manchester, 1936–46; Director of Economic Section 1941; Ministry of Aircraft Production 1941–4; Principal Assistant Secretary, Ministry of Reconstruction, 1944.

Kahn, Richard (later Lord): Fellow of King's College, Cambridge since 1931.

Keynes, J.M. : Fellow, King's College, Cambridge 1909–46, Treasury official 1915–19. Member of the Macmillan Committee and the Economic Advisory Council, and latter's Committee on Economic Information 1930–9. Economic adviser, Treasury, 1940–6.

Leith–Ross, Sir Frederick : Deputy Controller of Finance, Treasury

1925–32; Chief Economic Adviser to HM Government 1932–46 (Leith–Ross himself described the latter title as a misnomer, in that he was principally engaged in economic diplomacy).

Lloyd George, David : Prime Minister 1916–22. Leader of Liberal Party.

Meade, James : Fellow and Lecturer in Economics, Hertford College, Oxford 1930–7. Economic assistant, Economic Section, Cabinet Office 1940–5; Director 1945–7.

Niemeyer, Sir Otto : Controller of Finance, Treasury, 1922–7. Bank of England 1927–52.

Norman, Montagu (later Lord) : Governor of Bank of England 1920–44.

Phillips, Sir Frederick : Under Secretary, Treasury, 1932–9; Third Secretary 1939; represented Treasury in USA 1940–3.

Robbins, Professor Lionel : Professor of Economics, London School of Economics 1929–61. Director of Economic Section, Cabinet Office, 1941–5.

Rothbarth, Erwin : assistant in statistical research, Faculty of Economics and Politics, Cambridge University, 1938–40.

Rowan, Sir Leslie : Second Secretary, Treasury, 1947–9, 1951–8.

Snowden, Philip : Chancellor of the Exchequer 1924, 1929–31.

Stone, Sir Richard : served in Central Statistical Office, Offices of the War Cabinet, 1940–5. Director of Department of Applied Economics and Fellow of King's College, Cambridge, 1945.

Notes

1. A recent *select* collection of articles, *John Maynard Keynes: Critical Assessments*, ed. John Cunningham Graham (1983) ran to four volumes. There have, of course, also been many books written on the subject. The items in the bibliography of this pamphlet which are most useful to historians of economic thought are those by Chick [23], Corry [27], Hutchison [65] and Mehta [99].

2. *Hansard* (Commons), 5th series, ccxxvii, col. 54.

3. Thomas Jones, *Whitehall Diary*, ed. Keith Middlemas, vol. 2 (London, 1969), pp. 155–6.

4. Glynn and Howells [44] stress that the regional multiplier would be less than the national multiplier, owing to the fact that the depressed regions had a high propensity to import from other regions.

5. Evidence for this approach can be found in Public Record Office, London (hereafter, PRO), Treasury papers, series 175, file 117 (part 1) : Draft Statement on War Finance for the National Joint Advisory Council on 6 December 1939.

6. On these points see Kaldor, N., 'The 1941 White Paper on National Income and Expenditure', *Economic Journal*, lii (1942); Kalecki, M., 'The Budget and Inflation' and 'The Budget (1942–1943)' in Oxford University Institute of Statistics, *Studies in War Economics* (Oxford, 1947); Stone, R., 'The Use and Development of National Income and Expenditure Estimates', in D.N. Chester (ed.), *Lessons of the British War Economy* (Cambridge, 1951).

7. *The Times*, 27 May 1944, p. 5.

8. PRO, Cabinet Office Papers, series 87, volume 7 (Cab. 87/7): R (44) 6, Report of the Steering Committee on Post–War Employment.

9. Treasury scepticism is summed up in PRO, Cab 87/63: E.C. (43) 6, Memoranda prepared in the Treasury, 16 Oct. 1943.

References and Select Bibliography

Unless otherwise stated, the books were published in London. The abbreviation *EcHR* represents *Economic History Review*, second series.

[1] Addison, Paul, *The Road to 1945* (1975).
[2] Aldcroft, Derek, *The Inter-War Economy : Britain, 1919–1939* (1970).
[3] ——, 'British Monetary Policy and Economic Activity in the 1920s', *Revue internationale d'histoire de la banque*, v (1972).
[4] ——, *Full Employment : The Elusive Goal* (Brighton, 1984).
[5] Alford, B. W. E., *Depression and Recovery? British Economic Growth 1918–1939* (1972).
[6] Ashworth, William, *An Economic History of England, 1870–1939* (1960).
[7] Beveridge, William, *Social Insurance and Allied Services*, Cmd 6404 (1942).
[8] ——, *Full Employment in a Free Society* (1944). Keynes found himself in general agreement with this book, except for the chapter on international implications. See [89: *380–1*].
[9] Booth, Alan, 'The Second World War and the Origins of Modern Regional Policy', *Economy and Society*, xi (1982).
[10] ——, 'The "Keynesian Revolution" in Economic Policy-making', *EcHR*, xxxvi (1983). The conclusions of this article have been challenged by Rollings [127] and Tomlinson [144].
[11] Booth, Alan and Glynn, Sean, 'Unemployment in the Interwar Period: A Multiple Problem', *Journal of Contemporary History*, x (1975).
[12] Booth, Alan and Pack, Melvyn, *Employment, Capital and Economic Policy. Great Britain 1918–1939* (Oxford, 1985). A survey of ideas in the interwar period on how to deal with the slump. Keynes is shown to be the clearest thinker among the radicals.
[13] Bretherton, R. F., Burchardt, F. A. and Rutherford, R. S. G., *Public Investment and the Trade Cycle in Great Britain* (Oxford, 1941).
[14] Bridges, Edward, *Portrait of a Profession : The Civil Service Tradition* (Cambridge, 1950).
[15] ——, *Treasury Control* (1950).
[16] ——, *The Treasury* (1966). All three items by Bridges represent the ideas of an official who was in the Treasury or Cabinet Office throughout the period of the 'Keynesian revolution'.
[17] Buchanan, J. M., Burton, J. and Wagner, R. E., *The Consequences of Mr. Keynes* (1978).
[18] Burk, Kathleen, 'The Treasury : from Impotence to Power', in Kathleen Burk (ed.), *War and the State : The Transformation of British Government, 1914–1919* (1982).

[19] Cairncross, Alec, *Years of Recovery : British Economic Policy 1945–51* (1985). A major study based on archival research and perso‑ experience as an economic adviser.

[20] Cairncross, Alec and Eichengreen, Barry, S‑ ations of 1931, 1949 and 1967 (Oxford, 1983

[21] Casson, Mark, *Economics of Unemployment* (Oxford 1983). Helps to restore the reputati‑ who, unlike Keynes, were primarily concer‑ of real wages in relation to productivity, and mobility in the face of structural damages in

[22] Catterall, Ross, 'Attitudes to and the Impa‑ Policy in the 1920s', *Revue internationale d'histoire*

[23] Chick, Victoria, *Macroeconomics After Keynes:* *General Theory* (Deddington, 1983). An excellent ‑ ideas in terms of his original object in writing

[24] Clarke, Richard, *Anglo–American Economic Collabo‑* *1941–1949*, ed. Alec Cairncross (Oxford, 1982).

[25] Clarke, Peter, 'The Politics of Keynesian Economics, 1924–1931', in Michael Bentley and John Stevenson (eds), *High and Low Politics in Modern Britain* (Oxford, 1983). Concerned with political considerations which may have influenced Keynes during a crucial stage in his economic thought.

[26] Constantine, Stephen, *Unemployment in Britain between the Wars* (Harlow, 1980).

[27] Corry, B., 'Keynes in the History of Economic Thought', in A. P. Thirlwall (ed.), *Keynes and Laissez-Faire* (1978).

[28] Cunliffe Committee, *First Interim Report of the Committee on Currency and Foreign Exchanges after the War*, Cd 9182 (1918) and *Final Report*, Cmd. 464 (1919). Recommended a return to the gold standard. The *First Interim Report* contains a bland statement of the old orthodoxy.

[29] Cuyvers, Ludo, 'Keynes's Collaboration with Erwin Rothbarth', *Economic Journal*, XCIII (1983).

[30] Dimsdale, N. H., 'British Monetary Policy and the Exchange Rate 1920–38', *Oxford Economic Papers*, new series, XXXIII Supplement (1981).

[31] Dow, J. C. R., *The Management of the British Economy 1945–60* (Cambridge, 1964). Still the best work on domestic macroeconomic policy.

[32] Drummond, Ian, *The Floating Pound and the Sterling Area, 1931–1939* (Cambridge, 1981). A major work on economic diplomacy.

[33] Drummond, Ian, *The Gold Standard and the International Monetary System 1900–1939* (1986).

[34] *Economics of Full Employment* (Oxford, 1944). Keynes said there was scarcely a thing in it with which he did not agree, except for the section on international aspects. See [89: *381–3*].

[35] Eichengreen, Barry, 'Keynes and Protection', *Journal of Economic History*, XLIV (1984).

[36] *Employment Policy*, Cmd. 6527 (1944). Represents attempt by civil servants to reconcile new economic ideas with traditional canons of

public finance.

[37] Feinstein, Charles (ed.), *The Managed Economy : Essays in British Economic Policy and Performance since 1929* (Oxford, 1983).

[38] Gardiner, Richard N., *Sterling–Dollar Diplomacy* (New York, 1969). Standard account of the creation of the IMF and other post-war economic institutions, written without benefit of Keynes's own papers.

[39] Garside, W. R., 'The Failure of the "Radical Alternative" : Public Works, Deficit Finance and British Interwar Unemployment', *Journal of European Economic History* xiv (1985). Useful survey.

[40] Garside, W. R. and Hatton, T. J., 'Keynesian Policy and British Unemployment in the 1930s', *EcHR*, xxxviii (1985). A 'Keynesian' criticism of Glynn and Booth [41], based on optimistic assumptions of the short–run multiplier, price elasticities for exports and the mobility of labour.

[41] Glynn, Sean and Booth, Alan, 'Unemployment in Interwar Britain : A Case for Re–learning the Lessons of the 1930s?' *EcHR*, xxxvi (1983).

[42] ——, 'Building Counterfactual Pyramids', *EcHR*, xxxviii (1985). A response to Garside and Hatton [40].

[43] Glynn, Sean, Booth, Alan and Howells, Peter, 'NEH, NEH, NEH and the "Keynesian Solution"', *Australian Economic History Review*, xxv (1985). A response to Hatton [50].

[44] Glynn, Sean and Howells, P. G. A., 'Unemployment in the 1930s : The "Keynesian Solution" Reconsidered', *Australian Economic History Review*, xx (1980). Numerical exercise designed to show that it is naive to suppose that there was a simple Keynesian solution to unemployment in the 1930s. Broadly reinforces conclusions of Thomas [140], but challenged by Hatton [50].

[45] Grigg, P. J., *Prejudice and Judgement* (1948).

[46] Hall, R., 'The End of Full Employment', in Charles P. Kindleberger and Guido di Tella (eds), *Economics in the Long View* (1982), vol. 3.

[47] Harris, José, *William Beveridge, a Biography* (Oxford, 1977).

[48] Harrod, R. F., *The Life of John Maynard Keynes* (1951). Verges on hagiography, but still useful if one remembers that the author is a Keynesian economist.

[49] Hart, P. E., 'Macmillan Revisited', *Three Banks Review*, No 138 (1983). Brings out some of the major issues raised by evidence to Macmillan Committee.

[50] Hatton, T.J., 'Unemployment in the 1930s and the "Keynesian Solution" : Some Notes of Dissent', *Australian Economic History Review*, xxv (1985). Uses different assumptions and calculations from Glynn and Howells [44] to suggest that the impact of Keynesian policies would be more favourable on employment and on the budget than they allow.

[51] Hawtrey, R. G., 'The Gold Standard', *Economic Journal*, xxix (1919).

[52] ——, 'Public Expenditure and the Demand for Labour', *Economica*, v (1925).

[53] ——, *A Century of Bank Rate* (1938).

[54] ——, *Bretton Woods, For Better or Worse* (1946). Contemporary criticism of international monetary policy by an official who had just retired from the Treasury.

[55] Henderson, H. D., *The Inter-War Years and Other Papers*, edited by Henry Clay (Oxford, 1955). Includes memoranda prepared by Henderson while he was an economic adviser in the Treasury during the Second World War.

[56] Howson, Susan, ' "A Dear Money Man"? Keynes on Monetary Policy, 1920', *Economic Journal*, LXXXIII (1973).

[57] ——, 'The Origins of Dear Money, 1919–20', *EcHR*, XXVII (1974).

[58] ——, *Domestic Monetary Management in Britain 1919–38* (Cambridge, 1975). Major study of the evolution of Treasury's ideas. Based on extensive research in Treasury's records.

[59] ——, 'Monetary Theory and Policy in the 20th Century: the Career of R. G. Hawtrey', in Michael Flinn (ed.), *Proceedings of the Seventh International Economic History Congress* (Edinburgh, 1978).

[60] ——, *Sterling's Managed Float: The Operations of the Exchange Equalisation Account, 1932–39* (Princeton, 1980). A complementary work to her book on domestic monetary policy.

[61] ——, 'Slump and unemployment', in R. Floud and D. McCloskey (eds), *The Economic History of Britain since 1700*, vol. 2 (Cambridge, 1981).

[62] ——, 'Hawtrey and the Real World', in G. C. Harcourt (ed.), *Keynes and his Contemporaries* (1985). A study of the theories and influence of the only Treasury official in the interwar period to have a reputation as an economist.

[63] Howson, Susan and Winch, Donald, *The Economic Advisory Council, 1930–1939* (Cambridge, 1977). Seminal work dealing with relationship between economics and policy. For some critical comments see Peden [118].

[64] Hutchison, T. W., *Keynes versus the 'Keynesians' ...?* (1977). An essay on the thought of Keynes and the accuracy of its interpretation by his followers, with commentaries by Lord Kahn and Sir Austin Robinson.

[65] Hutchinson, T. W., *On Revolutions and Progress in Economic Knowledge* (Cambridge, 1978).

[66] Jewkes, John, 'The Government and Employment Policy : A Defence of the White Paper on Employment Policy', in John Jewkes, *A Return to Free Market Economics? Critical Essays on Government Intervention* (1978). Recollections and comments by one of the authors of the 1944 White Paper on *Employment Policy*.

[67] Johnson, Elizabeth, 'John Maynard Keynes : Scientist or Politician?' *Journal of Political Economy*, LXXXII (1974).

[68] Jones, M. E. F., 'The Regional Impact of an Overvalued Pound in the 1920s', *EcHR*, XXXVIII (1985).

[69] Jones, Russell, *Wages and Employment Policy, 1936–85* (1987). Important study of the development of thinking inside Whitehall on the problem of wage inflation in an economy at full employment.

[70] Kahn, R. F., 'The Relation of Home Investment to Unemployment', *Economic Journal*, XLI (1931).

[71] ——, 'Historical Origins of the International Monetary Fund', in A.P. Thirlwall (ed.), *Keynes and International Monetary Relations* (1976).

[72] ——, 'Unemployment as seen by the Keynesians', in G. D. N. Worswick (ed.), *The Concept and Measurement of Involuntary Unemployment* (1976).

[73] ——, *The Making of Keynes' General Theory* (Cambridge, 1984).

[74] Kaldor, N., 'Keynes as an Economic Adviser' in A. P. Thirlwall (ed.), *Keynes as a Policy Adviser* (1982).

[75] Keynes, J. M., *Collected Writings* (30 volumes, edited by Elizabeth Johnson or D. E. Moggridge). An invaluable source. The early volumes are standard editions of Keynes's major published works, while the later volumes contain much material hitherto unpublished or scattered through various journals and the press.

[76] ——, vol. 4, *A Tract on Monetary Reform* (1971).

[77] ——, vols 5 and 6, *A Treatise on Money* (1971).

[78] ——, vol. 7, *The General Theory of Employment, Interest and Money* (1973).

[79] ——, vol. 9, *Essays in Persuasion* (1972). Contains Keynes's pamphlets, *The Means to Prosperity* (1933) and *How to Pay for the War* (1940), which represent attempts by Keynes to explain his ideas at a level appropriate to a reader of *The Times*.

[80] ——, vol. 13, *The General Theory and After : Part I. Preparation* (1973).

[81] ——, vol. 14, *The General Theory and After : Part II. Defence and Development* (1973).

[82] ——, vol. 19, *Activities 1924–9 : The Return to Gold and Industrial Policy* (1981).

[83] ——, vol. 20, *Activities 1929–32 : Rethinking Employment and Unemployment Policies* (1981).

[84] ——, vol. 21, *Activities 1931–9 : World Crisis and Policies in Britain and America* (1982).

[85] ——, vol. 22, *Activities 1939–45 : Internal War Finance* (1978). Contains Keynes's ideas on how to apply the principles of *How to Pay for the War* (1940) in the 1941 and subsequent budgets.

[86] ——, vol. 24, *Activities 1944–6 : The Transition to Peace* (1979).

[87] ——, vol. 25, *Activities 1940–4 : Shaping the Post-War World : The Clearing Union* (1980).

[88] ——, vol. 26, *Activities 1943–6 : Shaping the Post-War World : Bretton Woods and Reparations* (1980).

[89] ——, vol. 27, *Activities 1940–6 : Shaping the Post-War World : Employment and Commodities* (1980). Contains Keynes's ideas between 1942 and 1946 on employment policy, including comments on the White Paper on *Employment Policy* (1944).

[90] Keynes, Milo (ed.), *Essays on John Maynard Keynes* (Cambridge, 1975).

[91] Leith-Ross, Frederick, *Money Talks : Fifty Years of International Finance* (1968).

[92] Little, I. M. D., 'Fiscal Policy', in G. D. N. Worswick and P. H. Ady (eds), *The British Economy 1945–1950* (Oxford, 1952).

[93] Lowe, Rodney, *Adjusting to Democracy : The Role of the Ministry of Labour in British Politics, 1916–1939* (Oxford, 1986).

[94] McCrone, Gavin, *Regional Policy in Britain* (1969).

[95] Macmillan Committee, *Report of the Committee on Finance and Industry*, Cmd 3897 (1931). Keynes dominated the proceedings of the Committee, both in examining witnesses and in drafting the report. See [83: *38–311*].

[96] May Committee, *Report of the Committee on National Expenditure*, Cmd 3920 (1931). Represents attempt to apply pre-Keynesian solution to economic crisis.

[97] Meade, J. E., *Planning and the Price Mechanism* (1948).

[98] ——, 'The Keynesian Revolution', in Milo Keynes (ed.), *Essays on John Maynard Keynes* (Cambridge, 1975). The best short account, as regards theory.

[99] Mehta, Ghanshyam, *The Structure of the Keynesian Revolution* (1977). Uses Kuhn's historiographical framework to argue that the decisive break with the classical tradition occurred in 1930, when Keynes published his *Treatise on Money*.

[100] *Memoranda on Certain Proposals Relating to Unemployment*, Cmd 3331 (1929). Arguments, prepared by civil servants from interested Whitehall departments, against public works proposals of Lloyd George and Keynes.

[101] Middleton, Roger, 'The Constant Employment Budget Balance and British Budgetary Policy 1929–39', *EcHR*, xxxiv (1981). Shows how far fiscal policy was from being reflationary until 1937/38.

[102] ——, 'The Treasury in the 1930s : Political and Administrative Constraints to Acceptance of the "New" Economics', *Oxford Economic Papers*, new series, xxxiv (1982).

[103] Middleton, Roger, 'The Treasury and Public Investment : A Perspective on Inter–war Economic Management', *Public Administration*, lxi (1983).

[104] ——, *Towards the Managed Economy : Keynes, the Treasury and the fiscal policy debate of the 1930s* (1985). A major study with Keynesian tendencies which nevertheless recognises some validity in Treasury arguments.

[105] Moggridge, D. E., *The Return to Gold 1925* (Cambridge, 1969). First version of a thesis subsequently amplified in [106].

[106] ——, *British Monetary Policy 1924–1931 : The Norman Conquest of $4.86* (Cambridge, 1972). A major study of how monetary policy was made.

[107] ——, 'Keynes the Economist', in D.E. Moggridge (ed.), *Keynes : Aspects of the Man and His Work* (1974).

[108] ——, *Keynes* (1976). Useful short study.

[109] Moggridge, D. E. and Howson, Susan, 'Keynes on Monetary Policy, 1910–1946', *Oxford Economic Papers*, new series, xxvi (1974).

[110] Morgan, E. V., *Studies in British Financial Policy, 1914–25* (1952).

[111] Patinkin, Don, 'Keynes and Econometrics: On the Interaction Between the Macroeconomic Revolutions of the Interwar Period',

Econometrica, xliv (1976). Illuminating survey of connections between Keynes's theory and preparation of national income estimates.

[112] ——, 'New Materials on the Development of Keynes' Monetary Thought', *History of Political Economy*, xii (1980).

[113] Peden, G. C., *British Rearmament and the Treasury, 1932–1939* (Edinburgh 1979). A case–study of the Treasury at work.

[114] ——, 'Keynes, the Treasury and Unemployment in the Later Nineteen–thirties', *Oxford Economic Papers*, new series, xxxii (1980).

[115] ——, 'Keynes, the Economics of Rearmament and Appeasement', in Wolfgang J. Mommsen and Lothar Kettenacker (eds), *The Fascist Challenge and the Policy of Appeasement* (1983).

[116] ——, 'Sir Richard Hopkins and the "Keynesian Revolution" in Employment Policy, 1929–45', *EcHR*, xxxvi (1983).

[117] ——, 'The Treasury as the Central Department of Government', *Public Administration*, lxi (1983).

[118] ——, 'The "Treasury View" on Public Works and Employment in the Interwar Period', *EcHR*, xxxvii (1984).

[119] ——, *British Economic and Social Policy : Lloyd George to Margaret Thatcher* (Deddington, 1985).

[120] Pimlott, Ben, *Hugh Dalton* (1985).

[121] Pollard, Sidney (ed.), *The Gold Standard and Employment Policies between the Wars* (1970). Useful collection, but editor's introduction places too much stress on importance of monetary policy.

[122] ——, *The Development of the British Economy 1914–1980* (1983).

[123] Pressnell, L. S., '1925 : The Burden of Sterling', *EcHR*, xxxi (1978).

[124] Redmond, John, 'An Indicator of the Effective Exchange Rate of the Pound in the Nineteen–thirties', *EcHR*, xxxiii (1980).

[125] ——, 'The Sterling Overvaluation in 1925 : A Multilateral Approach', *EcHR*, xxxvii (1984). The most recent attempt to quantify sterling's overvaluation under the restored gold standard.

[126] Robbins, Lionel, *Autobiography of an Economist* (1971).

[127] Rollings, N., 'The "Keynesian Revolution" and Economic Policy–making : A Comment', *EcHR*, xxxviii (1985). Well-researched contribution to the debate on Keynes's influence in the immediate postwar period. For further developments in the post-war period see Rollings's forthcoming article, 'British Budgetary Policy 1945–54 : A "Keynesian Revolution"?', *EcHR*.

[128] Roseveare, Henry, *The Treasury : The Evolution of a British Institution* (1969). A standard, but rather dated, work.

[129] Rowan, T. L., *Arms and Economics : The Changing Challenge* (Cambridge, 1960).

[130] Sayers, R. S., *Financial Policy 1939–1945* (1956). The chapter on the 1941 budget is reproduced in Feinstein [37].

[131] ——, 'The Return to Gold', in L. S. Pressnell (ed.), *Studies in the Industrial Revolution* (1960). Reprinted in Pollard [121].

[132] ——, *The Bank of England 1891–1944*, 3 vols (Cambridge, 1976).

[133] Skidelsky, Robert, *Oswald Mosley* (1975).

[134] ——, 'The reception of the Keynesian Revolution', in Milo Keynes (ed.), *Essays on John Maynard Keynes* (Cambridge, 1975).

[135] ——, 'Keynes and the Treasury View : the case for and against an Active Unemployment Policy in Britain 1920–1939', in W. J. Mommsen (ed.), *The Emergence of the Welfare State in Britain and Germany* (Beckenham, 1981). Contains valuable insights on the 1920s.

[136] ——, *John Maynard Keynes : Hopes Betrayed 1883–1920* (1983). The first volume in what promises to be a major biography.

[137] Stewart, Michael, *Keynes and After* (Harmondsworth, 1972). Dated as regards its assumptions about the significance of the Keynesian revolution, but contains an explanation of Keynes's economics in terms which are intelligible to the non-economist.

[138] Stone, Richard (ed.), *Inland Revenue Report on National Income 1929* (Cambridge, 1977).

[139] Thomas, Mark, 'Rearmament and Economic Recovery in the late 1930s' *EcHR*, xxxvi (1983).

[140] Thomas, T., 'Aggregate demand in the United Kingdom 1918–45', in Roderick Floud and Donald McCloskey (eds), *The Economic History of Britain since 1700*, vol. 2 (Cambridge, 1981). Important Keynesian reinterpretation of effectiveness of expansionary policies. Concludes that only by closing the economy, as Nazi Germany did, could Britain have carried out a successful employment policy based on deficit spending.

[141] Tomlinson, J., 'Unemployment and Government Policy Between the Wars : A Note', *Journal of Contemporary History*, xiii (1978).

[142] Tomlinson, J., *Problems of British Economic Policy 1870–1945* (1981). Attempts to define a 'Keynesian revolution', as he does in [143].

[143] ——, 'Why was there never a "Keynesian Revolution" in Economic Policy?', *Economy and Society*, x (1981).

[144] ——, 'A "Keynesian Revolution" in Economic Policy-Making?' *EcHR*, xxxvii (1984).

[145] ——, *British Macroeconomic Policy since 1940* (1985).

[146] Van Dormael, A., *Bretton Woods : Birth of a Monetary System* (1978). Most up-to-date account of negotiations, in which Keynes took a major part.

[147] Williamson, John, 'Keynes and the international economic order', in David Worswick and James Trevithick (eds), *Keynes and the Modern World : Proceedings of the Keynes Centenary Conference, King's College, Cambridge* (Cambridge, 1983). Useful short study.

[148] Williamson, Philip, 'Financiers, the Gold Standard and British Politics, 1925–1931', in John Turner (ed.), *Businessmen and Politics : Studies of Business Activity in British Politics 1900–1945* (1984). Contains much information.

[149] Wilson, T., 'Policy in War and Peace : The Recommendations of J. M. Keynes', in A. P. Thirlwall (ed.), *Keynes as a Policy Adviser* (1982). Quite the best short critique of Keynes on war finance and post-war employment policy.

[150] Winch, Donald, *Economics and Policy : A Historical Study* (1969). A very influential Keynesian interpretation.

Index